MUMMIES

AND THE SECRETS OF ANCIENT EGYPT

MUMMIES

AND THE SECRETS OF ANCIENT EGYPT

By
John Malam

Consultant
Dr. Joann Fletcher

A Dorling Kindersley Book

LONDON, NEW YORK, SYDNEY, DELHI,
PARIS, MUNICH, and JOHANNESBURG

Project Editor David John
Project Art Editor Joanna Pocock
Senior Editor Fran Jones
Senior Art Editor Marcus James
Category Publisher Jayne Parsons
Senior Managing Art Editor Jacquie Gulliver
US Editors Gary Werner, Margaret Parrish
Picture Researchers Angela Anderson, Nicole Kaczynsky, Bridget Tilley
Production Erica Rosen
DTP Designers Matthew Ibbotson, Louise Paddick

First American Edition, 2001

01 02 03 04 05 10 9 8 7 6 5 4 3 2 1

Published in the United States by
DK Publishing, Inc.
95 Madison Avenue
New York, New York 10016

Copyright © 2001 Dorling Kindersley Limited

CIP data is available from the Library of Congress

ISBN 0-7894-7975-3 (hc)
ISBN 0-7894-7976-1 (pb)

Reproduced by Colourscan, Singapore
Printed and bound by L.E.G.O., Italy

See our complete catalog at
www.dk.com

CONTENTS

6
INTRODUCTION

8
WHAT IS A MUMMY?

14
EGYPT – THE GIFT OF
THE NILE

20
EVERLASTING LIFE

24
ENTER THE GODS

30
WRAPPED FOR
ETERNITY

40
PYRAMID POWER

48
TOMB RAIDERS

52
THE PHARAOH –
GOD-KING OF EGYPT

58
TEMPLES – HOMES OF
THE GODS

62
MAGIC SPELLS AND
MEDICINE

66
EVERYDAY LIFE

76
IMAGES IN WRITING

82
ANIMAL MUMMIES

85
REFERENCE SECTION

94
INDEX

96
CREDITS

INTRODUCTION

Mummies, more than any other type of human remains, have the power to open windows onto lost worlds – and none more so than the mummies of ancient Egypt. These preserved people are unique pieces of evidence. They're not the oldest mummies in the world, nor are they always the best preserved, but they're the ones that cast the greatest spell over us.

Mummies are the product of an age-old human desire – to survive death and allow the soul to live forever by preventing the body's decay. Whether this ever succeeded no one can say, but one thing's certain – fascination with mummies has kept them alive in the popular imagination. When we study past civilizations we tend to look at the remains of their monuments,

THE WORLD WENT MUMMY-MAD WITH THE DISCOVERY OF TUTANKHAMUN'S TOMB IN 1922.

writing, and other objects that have survived. But the mummy of a person who died long ago is often far more interesting than anything else an archaeologist might dig up. The reason for this is simple – a person who lived and died in the past can help piece together the

ANUBIS, THE JACKAL-HEADED GOD OF EMBALMING, ANOINTS A YOUNG MAN.

past. Their bones, teeth, flesh, vital organs, skin, hair, and fingernails hold amazing secrets about the time and place in which they lived. Today, advances in modern technology, such as X-rays, radio-carbon dating, and DNA analysis, are allowing us to unravel some of these mysteries for the first time.

This book tells the story of ancient Egypt and its mummies. You'll find out about the Egyptians' everyday lives, their strange gods, magic beliefs, and powerful pharaohs. You'll be guided through their massive stone buildings – their pyramids, temples, and tombs. You'll also discover how the Egyptians perfected the art of embalming, and how their mummies can help us to understand one of the greatest civilizations the world has ever known.

For those of you who want to explore the subject in more detail, there are Log On "bites" that appear throughout the book. These will direct you to some fascinating websites where you can check out even more about ancient Egypt.

John Malam

WHAT IS A MUMMY?

You've probably opened this book because you want to find out the grisly truth about mummies. But which mummies are those, exactly? Are they the ones from Egypt or China, from South America or northern Europe? The fact is that mummies come from all over the world; it just happens that the ones from ancient Egypt are the most famous of them all.

THIS COFFIN CONTAINED THE MUMMY OF AN EGYPTIAN PRIESTESS.

Preserved people

At one time, every mummy was a flesh and blood person – a living human being. One day that person curled up his or her toes and died. Throughout human history, in every civilization on Earth, dead bodies have been buried in the ground where they became worm food. Others were burned until they turned to ash. But a small number of bodies have been preserved.

It may sound creepy, but some ancient corpses, which can be thousands of years old, look so fresh you'd think they were asleep. For them, time has stood still. For us, they're time capsules.

Mummified people open a window on the past, and through them we can learn about the societies they came from. It is as if their voices can be heard again, speaking to us from long ago.

Mummified by accident
Most mummies in ancient Egypt were deliberately made. The Egyptian embalmers wanted to make their customers' dead bodies last forever. But elsewhere in the world,

TOLLUND MAN WAS FOUND IN A PEAT BOG IN DENMARK. HE DIED 2,000 YEARS AGO.

BODIES HAVE BEEN FROZEN, DRIED OUT, EVEN PICKLED!

SCIENTISTS REFROZE THIS 5,300-YEAR-OLD ICEMAN IN A GIANT FRIDGE BECAUSE HE WAS BEGINNING TO THAW!

some bodies became mummies by accident – there was no special embalming (preserving) treatment for them.

You probably wouldn't think of looking in a glacier, or a peat bog, to find a mummy. But it's in these unlikely places that some of the most magnificent mummies have been found.

Ice man and bog man

In 1991, tourists found the dried-out body of a young man frozen in a glacier on a mountain between Austria and Italy. He died in this bleak place 5,300 years ago, and the ice preserved him like meat in a freezer.

Bodies can even be preserved in places that contain very little oxygen, like marshy bogs. It's oxygen that makes flesh rot and iron rust.

The people who lived in northern Europe about 2,000 years ago, didn't know this. They threw sacrifice

MUMMIES IN PERU WERE BOUND WITH ROPE. THIS MUMMY HAS BEEN UNWRAPPED.

victims and criminals into peat bogs. The conditions in these cold, airless, watery places were perfect for pickling bodies – their skin turned into leather. Peat-harvesters have found these bog bodies in England, Germany, and Denmark.

The first mummy-makers

The ancient Egyptians were not the first people to mummify their dead.

That claim to fame belongs to the people of southern Peru and northern Chile, who, 10,000 years ago, began to bury corpses in the sand of the Atacama Desert. It was there, in one of the world's driest places, that human tissue was first mummified naturally by the environment. When the local people found that their dearly departed were not rotting in the ground, they developed methods of artifical mummification. From about 5000 BC, they began to strip the skin from their dead and remove the internal organs.

When a body was dry it was "rebuilt" with sticks, reeds, animal hair, paste, and paint. The end result was a stuffed and painted mummy that looked more like a doll than a person.

LOG ON...
www.mummytombs.com/main.welcome.htm

Mummies in Asia

Deserts in other parts of the world have also produced "crops"

> **WEIRD WORLD**
> ICE MUMMY JOHN TORRINGTON DIDN'T DIE FROM COLD, BUT FROM LEAD POISONING. SOUP CANS ON HIS SHIP HAD BEEN SEALED WITH LEAD.

TORRINGTON, AN ENGLISH SAILOR, WAS LEFT ON THE ARCTIC ICE IN 1845. HIS CREW WAS LOOKING FOR THE NORTHWEST PASSAGE.

of mummies. In China's Taklamakan Desert there is a cemetery that was in use for 1,500 years, from about 1800 BC to 300 BC. The dried-out bodies found there have puzzled scientists because they look like European people, not Asian. Who were they? What were they doing there? The answer seems to be that they were settlers who had traveled to Asia from Europe. No one knew anything about them until their well-preserved mummies were found.

Asia has frozen mummies, too. About 2,500 years ago, nomads called the Pazyryk lived in the icy wastes of

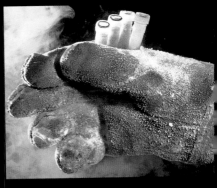

MODERN SCIENCE USES ULTRA-LOW TEMPERATURES TO PRESERVE HUMAN TISSUE, FROM WHOLE BODIES TO JUST A FEW CELLS.

Siberia. Their dead leaders were buried in deep graves covered by mounds of soil. Inside, their bodies were protected by the region's severe cold. From one of these graves, or kurgans, came a woman now known as the Ice Princess. Her body was decorated with

AN EGYPTIAN MUMMY, STILL INSIDE ITS COFFIN, ENTERS A BODY SCANNER. THE SCANNER EXAMINES THE INSIDES.

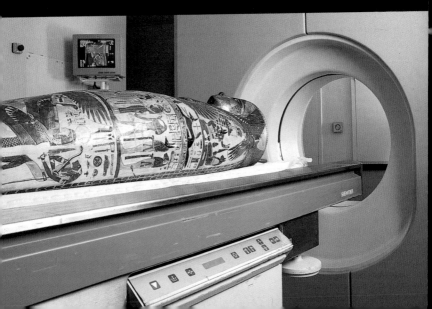

tattoos, and she had been buried in her finest clothes.

Egyptian mummies

Among the world's mountain of mummies, it's the ones from ancient Egypt that were the most elaborately preserved. Skilled embalmers used knives and hooks, salts and perfumes, packing and bandages to prepare a body for everlasting life. And not just human bodies, either! If it had a heartbeat, the Egyptians mummified it. Cats, dogs, birds, fish, snakes, mice, and even beetles were mummified if they were needed as pets in the afterlife, or if they represented certain gods.

At first, Egyptian mummies were made by accident. The earliest Egyptians buried their dead in pits dug into the land's hot, dry sand. The bodies dried out, and Egypt's first mummies were "born." But when we think of Egyptian mummies it's the ones carefully wrapped in bandages that come to mind. These "true" mummies were made from at least 2600 BC.

Learning from mummies

Not so long ago, scientists used to unwrap and cut open mummies to find out about a person's age, health, diet, and what they died from. This is rarely done now. Today's scientists use technology such as X-rays, body scanners, radio-carbon dating, and DNA analysis to learn about people from the past. These methods of research are nondestructive, which means the mummies are left in good shape. That's important, because once a mummy was a real person – someone who hoped that when

THE SANDS WILL RISE. THE HEAVENS WILL PART. THE POWER WILL BE UNLEASHED.

FROM THE EARLIEST DAYS OF SILENT SILVER SCREEN CINEMA TO TODAY'S SPECIAL-EFFECTS BLOCKBUSTERS, MUMMIES HAVE BEEN MADE INTO MOVIE STARS.

they died their body would be left in peace. Today's scientists respect the dead, which is why they do as little as possible to disturb a mummy's sleep.

EGYPT – THE GIFT OF THE NILE

The civilization of ancient Egypt lasted for more than 3,000 years. It flourished along a thin strip of fertile land that lay on each side of the Nile River. For the people who lived there, this great river brought life and prosperity. Their land was "the gift of the Nile," and their magnificent culture became one of the greatest the world has ever known.

Egypt's great highway

The Nile River is the world's longest river, flowing north for some 4,145 miles (6,740 km) from its source in Burundi, East Africa, to the Mediterranean Sea. The civilization of ancient Egypt owed its very existence to this mighty, life-giving river. The Nile watered the land, and crops grew in abundance along its banks. It was also easy to navigate and provided a highway between the upper and lower parts of the country. The river's flood plain was narrow, ranging between

THE EASIEST WAY TO TRAVEL IN EGYPT IS BY RIVER. THAT'S AS TRUE FOR US AS IT WAS FOR THE ANCIENT EGYPTIANS.

1–25 miles (2–40 km) wide, and it was along this thin green belt of land that the ancient Egyptians lived.

The Nile in flood

Every year, summer rains in the mountains at the source of the Nile caused the river to burst

THIS IS EGYPT SEEN FROM SPACE. YOU CAN SEE THE NILE WINDING ITS WAY TOWARD YOU FROM ITS SOURCE IN EAST AFRICA.

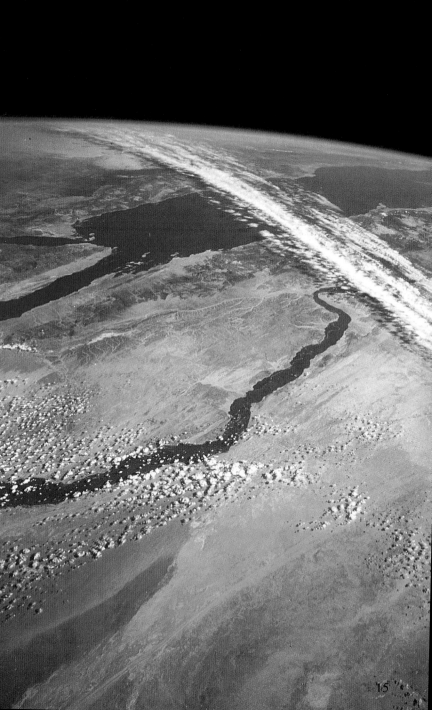
15

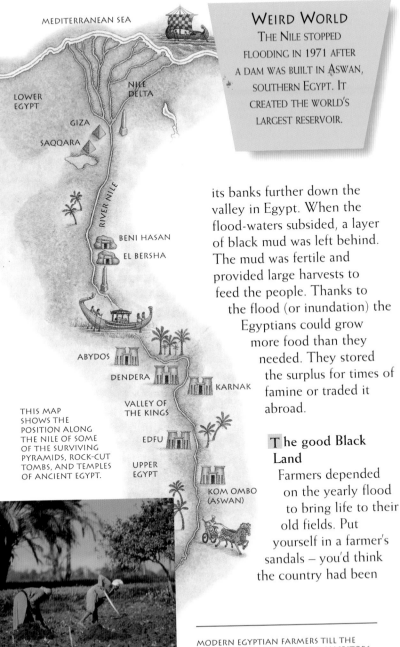

MEDITERRANEAN SEA

NILE DELTA

LOWER EGYPT

GIZA

SAQQARA

RIVER NILE

BENI HASAN

EL BERSHA

ABYDOS

DENDERA

KARNAK

VALLEY OF THE KINGS

THIS MAP SHOWS THE POSITION ALONG THE NILE OF SOME OF THE SURVIVING PYRAMIDS, ROCK-CUT TOMBS, AND TEMPLES OF ANCIENT EGYPT.

EDFU

UPPER EGYPT

KOM OMBO (ASWAN)

its banks further down the valley in Egypt. When the flood-waters subsided, a layer of black mud was left behind. The mud was fertile and provided large harvests to feed the people. Thanks to the flood (or inundation) the Egyptians could grow more food than they needed. They stored the surplus for times of famine or traded it abroad.

The good Black Land

Farmers depended on the yearly flood to bring life to their old fields. Put yourself in a farmer's sandals – you'd think the country had been

MODERN EGYPTIAN FARMERS TILL THE BLACK SOIL EXACTLY AS THEIR ANCESTORS DID IN THE TIME OF THE PHARAOHS.

born again because the squelchy black mud dumped by the Nile was new land. The Egyptians lived their lives around this yearly cycle and even named their country after the mud. Their word for Egypt was *Kemet*, which means "Black Land." To them, black was a good color, and *Kemet* was a land of plenty. No wonder they called themselves *remetch en Kemet* – "the people of the Black Land."

EGYPT WOULD NOT EXIST WITHOUT THE NILE. ITS BANKS ARE LUSH AND FERTILE, BUT BEYOND THIS LIE VAST SANDY DESERTS.

the Sun set in the west. At dusk, it sank slowly from sight, as if it were being extinguished and swallowed by the desert.

WHEN THE NILE FLOODED, THE PEOPLE SAW THEIR LAND REBORN

The bad Red Land

Beyond the narrow fertile strip was a vast, sandy desert. The ancient Egyptians called the desert *Deshret*, meaning "Red Land." To their way of thinking, the dry, red sand of *Deshret* was a place of death – it was the complete opposite of *Kemet*.

What's more, the desert in the west was said to be the entrance to the underworld, the kingdom of the dead. As if to make the link between the desert and death even clearer,

A land of opposites

Ancient Egypt was a land of two very different parts – one part wet and fertile where nearly everyone lived, and one part dry and barren where almost no one lived. The ancient Egyptians were great believers in what we call "duality," the idea that everything has an exact opposite, like good and evil, living and dead. This idea of opposites crops up time and again in the ancient Egyptian world.

17

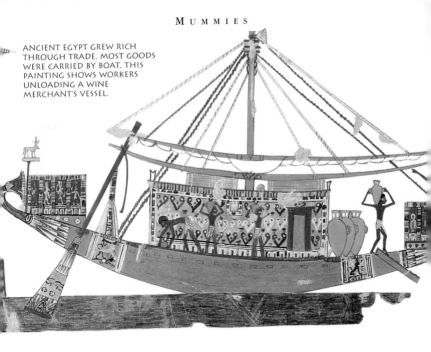

ANCIENT EGYPT GREW RICH THROUGH TRADE. MOST GOODS WERE CARRIED BY BOAT. THIS PAINTING SHOWS WORKERS UNLOADING A WINE MERCHANT'S VESSEL.

The opposite of Egypt

The ancient Egyptians believed that Egypt itself had a heavenly opposite in the afterlife. This was where all Egyptians longed to travel after death – to a perfect world where they would enjoy eternal life. Belief in the afterlife was so strong that the ancient Egyptians went to extraordinary lengths to prepare for it. The most important preparation was to preserve the dead body, especially the face, in a lifelike way. This was crucial if a dead person's spirit was to recognize its old body after death. If the spirit couldn't find its body when it returned to the tomb, everlasting life would not begin. Preparations for the journey after death were also elaborate. Tombs were crammed with everything the Egyptians thought they might need in the afterlife – and they did not travel light!

Our knowledge of Egypt

Many clues to Egypt's past have disappeared. Thieves have stolen treasures. Desert sands and time itself have worn away the ancient villages and cities. But still we know a great deal about the ancient Egyptians.

THIS GIANT STATUE OF PHARAOH RAMESSES II (REIGNED 1279–13 BC) SHOWS HIM WEARING THE DUAL CROWN OF EGYPT – A SYMBOL OF THE UNITY OF THE TWO LANDS.

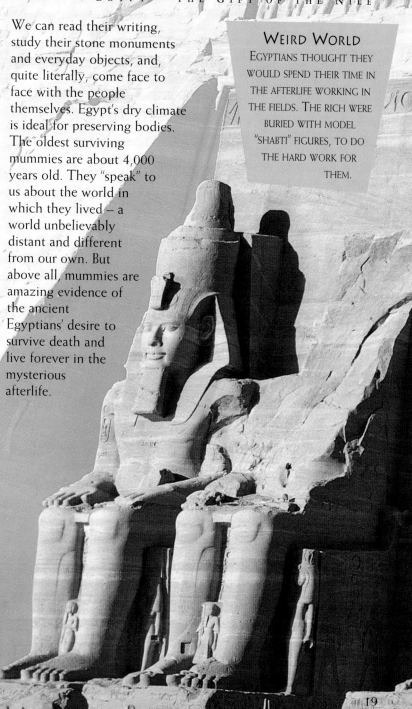

We can read their writing, study their stone monuments and everyday objects, and, quite literally, come face to face with the people themselves. Egypt's dry climate is ideal for preserving bodies. The oldest surviving mummies are about 4,000 years old. They "speak" to us about the world in which they lived – a world unbelievably distant and different from our own. But above all, mummies are amazing evidence of the ancient Egyptians' desire to survive death and live forever in the mysterious afterlife.

WEIRD WORLD

EGYPTIANS THOUGHT THEY WOULD SPEND THEIR TIME IN THE AFTERLIFE WORKING IN THE FIELDS. THE RICH WERE BURIED WITH MODEL "SHABTI" FIGURES, TO DO THE HARD WORK FOR THEM.

19

EVERLASTING LIFE

The ancient Egyptians' idea of heaven was a garden paradise. They called it the Field of Reeds – a place where the sun shone, and people worked happily harvesting crops. It was very similar to Egypt, except that the grain grew much taller, and everything was perfect! But the journey to the afterlife was full of danger, and passed through the underworld – an ordeal for which every Egyptian wanted to be prepared.

The cycle of life

According to the ancient Egyptians, life was a series of changes. You entered this world as a baby. As time passed the baby changed into a child, and then into an adult. The final change came with death. The Egyptians didn't think

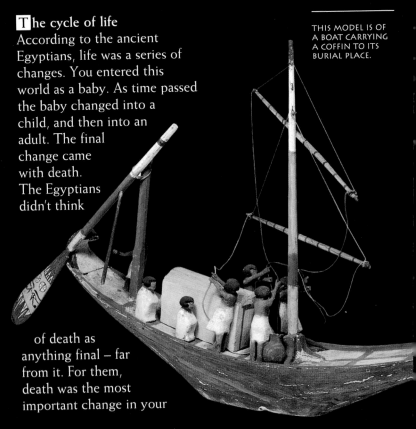

THIS MODEL IS OF A BOAT CARRYING A COFFIN TO ITS BURIAL PLACE.

of death as anything final – far from it. For them, death was the most important change in your

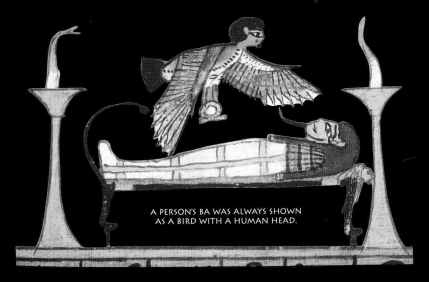

A PERSON'S BA WAS ALWAYS SHOWN
AS A BIRD WITH A HUMAN HEAD.

cycle of life. It marked the point at which you began another existence in a better place. Their way of describing

snakes and lakes of fire. A simple coffin wasn't protection enough against dangers such as these, so the Egyptians made

IN ANCIENT EGYPT, DEATH WAS THE FINAL LEG OF A JOURNEY

death was "the night of going forth to life." But before you could reach the afterlife, there was a long and terrifying journey to make through the underworld and an examination of your past life.

The Book of the Dead
Parts of the underworld were full of horrors, such as deadly

sure they were armed with hundreds of magic spells to help them through. These came from an ancient work called the Book of the Dead. Spells were written on the coffin or on a scroll tucked in with the mummy, together with a map of the underworld. The book was your passport. If you could recite the correct spells, you might get through unharmed.

21

The hall of Two Truths

The ultimate danger in the underworld was failing the test set for you in the hall of Two Truths. This was where your heart was weighed against a feather, the symbol of truth, to see if you deserved everlasting life. The jackal-headed god Anubis presented you before a jury of gods, who accused you of crimes committed during your life, which you denied. If your denial was true, the god of wisdom, Thoth, wrote that you were "true of voice" and let you through to the afterlife, where you lived forever. An awful punishment awaited if you were untruthful. Your heart was thrown to the crocodile-headed goddess Ammut, called "the devourer of the dead," who sat behind Thoth.

The two spirits

The Egyptians believed that everyone possessed certain spirit forms, which were released from the body

THE MOST IMPORTANT MOMENT IN A MUMMY'S "LIFE" IS THIS CEREMONY BEFORE THE GOD ANUBIS. HERE, A DEAD MAN'S HEART IS WEIGHED AGAINST THE FEATHER OF TRUTH.

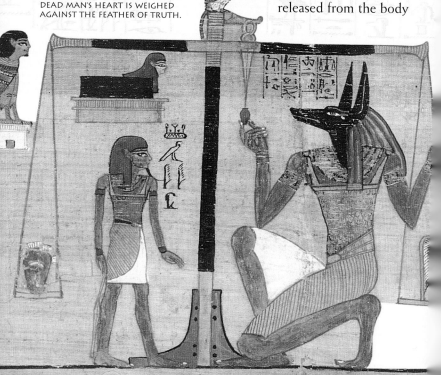

after death. The main ones were called the *ka* and the *ba*.

The *ka* was your "invisible twin" and your life force. While you were alive the *ka* lived only inside your body. But at the moment of death it was free to come and go as it wished. It still used the body as its home, and this is why preserving the body was so important. The *ka* also needed food and drink, which were provided through offerings or images of food placed in the tomb.

The *ba* was your personality. It was all the things that made you the way you were. The *ba* could eat, speak, and even visit the land of the living. It was usually pictured as a bird with a human head. To live forever, your *ka* and *ba* had to be reunited in the tomb with your mummy. Once this happened, you would become immortal. But before you could hope for everlasting life, you had to spend this life being careful not to offend any of ancient Egypt's numerous gods.

WEIRD WORLD
TOMB WALLS OFTEN HAD FALSE DOORS. THESE WERE MEANT AS GATEWAYS FOR THE SPIRIT TO TRAVEL BETWEEN THE WORLDS OF THE LIVING AND THE DEAD.

THOTH, THE GOD OF WISDOM, TAKES NOTES AS THE HEART IS WEIGHED. THE GODDESS AMMUT SITS BEHIND HIM.

ENTER THE GODS

The ancient Egyptians had a bewildering number of gods. There may even have been as many as 2,000. Many gods appear in several different forms, so it's often difficult to work out who's who. Over time, some gods grew in importance, and others declined. In the end, of course, they all lost their power and died out as Egyptian religious beliefs changed. But the gods' mysterious natures, tall crowns, and animal heads, continue to fascinate and haunt.

AMUN-RA WAS THE KING OF THE GODS. HE WORE A CROWN OF TALL FEATHERS.

Gods local and personal

Most of ancient Egypt's gods were minor figures worshipped in only a few towns and villages. Deities that fit into this group are called local gods. Other deities were personal gods. These were ones chosen by an individual for reasons best known only to that person.

For example, if you decided that the snake living in the hole outside your house is a god in the form of a snake, you'd look after it. You'd build a shrine in the snake's honour, leave it food, and offer prayers. In return, your god would protect you...you hoped!

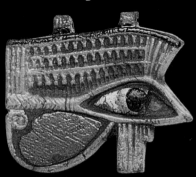

THE WEDJAT EYE WAS A COMMON AMULET. IT REPRESENTED THE EYE OF HORUS, AND WAS WORN FOR PROTECTION.

shown with human bodies and the heads of animals, birds, or

In the evening, he took the form of a ram. Thoth, the god

insects, depending on which one represented their power. Some had a variety of animal forms. For example, at dawn the sun-god was shown as Khepri, the scarab-beetle, rolling the sun disk above the eastern horizon. Later in the

of scribes and learning, was sometimes shown as a baboon, and at other times as an ibis.

Other gods, such as Anubis, with a jackal's head, or Osiris,

OSIRIS WAS THE GOD OF THE UNDERWORLD. HIS KINGDOM WAS THE GHOSTLY "OPPOSITE" OF EARTHLY EGYPT.

with his green face, are easier to recognize! Today, some of these gods may appear bizarre and even scary, but to the Egyptians they were like old familiar friends.

The gods of power

The gods and goddesses that mattered most were the universal deities – dynamic beings with fantastic powers and important jobs to do. They were the gods whose statues and pictures were everywhere, and whom people loved or dreaded.

Great temples were built for these deities, who were worshipped throughout the land as part of the official, or state, religion of Egypt. These gods were the immortals who brought order into the world. Without them the world would be in total chaos, so everyone thought.

WEIRD WORLD

EVER SEEN A SNAIL-LIKE FOSSIL CALLED AN AMMONITE? IT GETS ITS NAME FROM AMMON, THE GREEK NAME FOR AMUN. AMMONITES WERE SO-NAMED BECAUSE THEY LOOKED LIKE THE CURLY RAM'S HORNS OF AMMON.

OSIRIS WAS SHOWN WITH A GREEN FACE, SYMBOLIZING EGYPT'S PLANT LIFE, AND REBIRTH.

26

R a and Amun

Ra (also called Re) was for a long time the most important god of all. He was the sun god, the god upon whom all life on earth depended. He was the shining sun itself. Closely linked with Ra was Amun. At first he was worshipped as a local god in Thebes, the ancient capital of Egypt; but as Thebes became more important, so too did Amun. In time, he became the creator god, the god who was said to have created all the other gods. As his powers changed, so did his name. Because of his links with Ra, his name became Amun-Ra.

O siris and Isis

One of the most-loved gods was Osiris. He had triumphed over death, and every Egyptian wanted to follow his example. Osiris was the god of rebirth. He was also the ruler of the underworld.

Far back in history, Osiris was said to have been a good pharaoh who brought civilization to Egypt. When he took his sister Isis as his queen, he was killed by his jealous

ISIS IS SHOWN HERE HOLDING HER SON, HORUS. AS "MISTRESS OF MAGIC," ISIS EVENTUALLY BECAME THE MOST POWERFUL OF ALL THE GODS.

brother Seth, the god of chaos, storms, and war. Seth chopped Osiris' body into pieces and scattered them throughout Egypt. Isis collected the pieces and made them into the first mummy. Osiris was then reborn, and lived on to rule the dead. He was the first king to survive death. Through believing in Osiris, and the story of his rebirth, people hoped they, too, would have life after death.

H orus

Isis's son by Osiris was Horus, the god of the sky. When Horus grew up, he avenged his father's murder by killing Seth, and taking the throne of Egypt. But during the battle with Seth he lost an eye. The Eye of Horus, or *Wedjat* Eye, became a symbol of victory over evil.

A nubis

There's a doglike animal in Egypt that has a habit of prowling around cemeteries at

27

night. It's the jackal, and because of its liking for the places where the ancient Egyptians buried their dead, it became associated with death itself. For this reason the jackal was treated with respect. If you scared a jackal, or threw stones

THE JACKAL WAS LINKED TO DEATH BECAUSE OF ITS TASTE FOR CORPSES

and harmed it, people thought it would get its revenge by digging the dead from their graves – and eating them! It was because of the jackal's taste for corpses that Anubis, a god with the head of a jackal, became the god who made the dead ready for burial.

The daddy of mummies

Anubis was the god of mummy-making. It was his job to preserve a body for eternity. According to legend, the first body Anubis helped mummify was that of Osiris.

The face of Anubis was usually shown painted black. This was the color of the fertile mud left by the flooding of the Nile River. Mud represented the rebirth of the land, and mummification was the process of being reborn.

BASTET, THE CAT GODDESS, WAS THE DAUGHTER OF RA. SHE REPRESENTED THE POWER OF THE SUN TO RIPEN CROPS.

THIS PAINTING OF ANUBIS SHOWS HIM MUMMIFYING THE BODY OF A PHARAOH.

WRAPPED FOR ETERNITY

Mummy-making was perfected in a land that had plenty of the ingredients needed to preserve a body naturally – heat and sand. Egypt's hot, dry climate seemed to preserve buried corpses, and even keep them looking lifelike. This made the ancient Egyptians wonder whether they could preserve bodies for the afterlife. Once they'd discovered how to stop a corpse from rotting, the mummy-makers set to refining their fabulous craft.

EVEN THE EARLIEST SAND MUMMIES WERE BURIED WITH GOODS FOR THE AFTERLIFE, LIKE JEWELRY.

The mummy age

Throughout the vast era of ancient Egyptian history, one thing never changed. This was the powerful belief that a person would live forever in the afterlife if their body was somehow preserved. As the centuries passed, Egyptian mummy-makers continually improved their embalming techniques in order to make everlasting life a reality.

As a result, mummies were made in Egypt for about 3,000 years.

HOT, DRY, DESERT SAND PRESERVED BURIED BODIES AND PREVENTED THEM FROM DECAYING.

30

The first ones were made around 2600 BC and the last ones around AD 400.

The first Egyptian mummies

Long before the ancient Egyptians started to make mummies, nature was doing it for them. In the time before 2600 BC, the dead were buried in shallow pits scooped into the desert sand, surrounded by goods for the afterlife. But their peace was often short-lived. Grave robbers dug into the pits to steal valuable items made from gold and lapis lazuli, a dark blue stone used for jewelry.

To the robbers' horror and amazement, they found that some bodies still looked lifelike, curled up as if they were asleep, not dead. The bodies' juices had leaked away into the desert sand, leaving the flesh and skin hard and leathery. The hot, sandy conditions had completely dried them out.

RICH MUMMIES HAD BANDAGES MADE FROM THE CLOTHES USED TO DRESS STATUES OF THE GODS IN TEMPLES.

Stopping the rot

Perhaps it was the discovery of these dried-out bodies that made the ancient Egyptians think in a new way about life after death. They began reasoning that if a dead person was to be reborn, and live again, the person's body had to

WEIRD WORLD

NOTHING USED IN THE EMBALMING PROCESS WAS THROWN AWAY. TOOLS AND EVEN HAIR AND NAIL CLIPPINGS WERE BURIED WITH THE MUMMY.

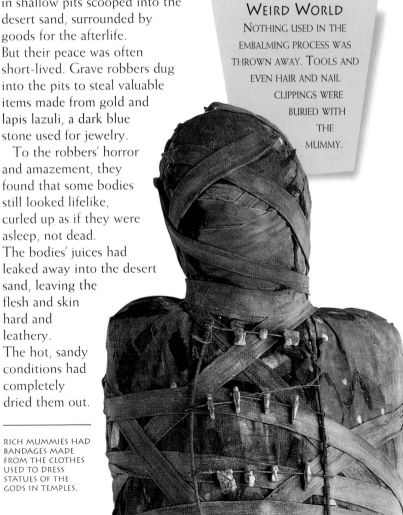

be preserved. It would become a "home" for the body's spirits (the *ka* and the *ba*).

The desert bodies proved that the natural process of decay could be stopped. And so, the search began for a way of preserving bodies artificially through embalming. But it wasn't until an era of Egyptian history known as the New Kingdom (c.1550–1070 BC) that the embalmers really perfected their art. So what did embalmers do?

A MUMMY'S WRAPPING WAS COMPLETED WITH A LARGE SHEET CALLED A SHROUD. SHROUDS WERE COATED IN MIXTURES OF RESIN, WAX, AND PERFUME.

B rain drain

They began by removing the brain. Long hooks made from bronze were pushed up through the nostrils and the hole at the base of the skull where it joins the spine. The hooks were then whisked round inside the skull until the brain was a soupy liquid that could be pulled and

THE PROCESS OF WRAPPING A MUMMY TOOK ABOUT 15 DAYS

A bloody business

Embalmers worked in open-air tents, close to the Nile River. They chose these places because they needed plenty of water to wash and clean the dead bodies. They probably also wanted plenty of fresh air to blow away the bad smells rising from their trade! When a grieving family brought a dead "customer" to the embalmers, the body was laid out on a flat wooden or stone table. The family was told to come back in 70 days, and the embalmers got to work.

drained from the head through the nostrils. When the skull was empty it was filled with a hot gooey fluid made from tree resin, bee's wax, and sweet-smelling plant oils. As it cooled, it set hard.

R emoving the insides

Next, the embalmers started on the person's tummy area. A deep cut was made on the left side of the abdomen through which the organs were removed. Out came the lungs, liver, stomach, and intestines.

Each was then wrapped in linen bandages and packed into separate pots known as canopic jars. The heart was left inside the body, because the Egyptians believed it controlled a person's intelligence and emotions.

Preserving salt

The body was now a gutless, brainless, empty shell, and was ready to be dried out. After washing the abdomen and chest cavity clean, it was packed with a natural, salty substance called natron. This was collected from the edges of

THE FINE GOLD ON THIS NEST OF COFFIN CASES INDICATES THAT ITS MUMMY WAS SOMEONE VERY IMPORTANT.

lakes. Natron did the same job as the hot sand of the desert – it absorbed water and other liquids. It also stopped the spread of mold and fungi, and acted as an antiseptic that killed destructive bacteria. After being packed with natron, the body was then completely covered in a big pile of it and left for 40 days.

When the natron had done its job, the body was dried out. It was a ghastly sight! The skin was dark and blotchy all over, and the legs were thin, like matchsticks. It was time for the embalmers to use their expert cosmetic skills to give the body a lifelike appearance.

The natural look

First, the abdomen and chest were packed with linen, sawdust, and even mud to give the body shape. Sweet-smelling oils were then rubbed into the skin to make it soft and supple. The nostrils, ears, and mouth were plugged with wads of linen. The eyes were pushed down into the head and balls of

linen were popped into the empty sockets. Then the eyelids were pulled down over the eyes to give them a sleeping appearance.

Usually, the cut in the abdomen was sealed with wax. However, if the person was very important, a thin sheet of gold might be placed over the ugly-looking gash.

Last of all, a layer of molten resin was poured over the body to harden it up and make it waterproof. All this made the body look natural again.

Wrapping up

With the embalming process over, it was time to wrap the body in layers of bandages. Thin strips of linen were used, often torn from worn-out

> **WEIRD WORLD**
> WHEN ALEXANDER THE GREAT DIED IN 323 BC, HIS BODY WAS EMBALMED WITH HONEY AND PLACED ON DISPLAY IN A GLASS COFFIN FOR ALL TO SEE.

THE EMBALMERS DID A SUPERB JOB ON RAMESSES II. THEY KEPT HIS BIG NOSE IN SHAPE BY STUFFING IT WITH PEPPERCORNS!

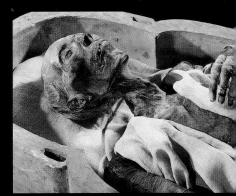

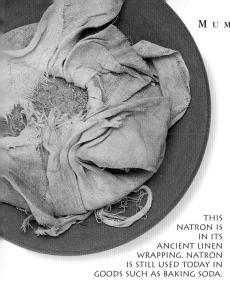

THIS NATRON IS IN ITS ANCIENT LINEN WRAPPING. NATRON IS STILL USED TODAY IN GOODS SUCH AS BAKING SODA.

clothes and furnishings. The body was wrapped in layer after layer, covering it from head to toe. During the wrapping process, priests chanted prayers and spells. Magic charms, called amulets, and jewelry were placed between the layers of bandages. These were to protect the person from harm during the long and difficult journey into the afterlife.

Once the body was covered in linen, the family would not see any mistakes the embalmers might have made. There are examples of a head that snapped off, then was attached to the neck with a stick, and a queen whose face was so well stuffed with pads of linen that her cheeks burst open!

Coffins

About 70 days after a person's death, their mummy was put inside a wooden coffin. For greater protection, it was sometimes placed inside a "nest" of several coffins, each colorfully decorated with spells to ward off evil. For real, heavy-duty protection, given to the wealthy, the coffins were sealed inside a massive stone container called a sarcophagus, which could weigh several tons. All this helped the dead person through the terrors of

THIS FEMALE MUMMY IS PROTECTED BY DOZENS OF AMULETS. MANY ARE STILL HIDDEN AMONG HER BANDAGES.

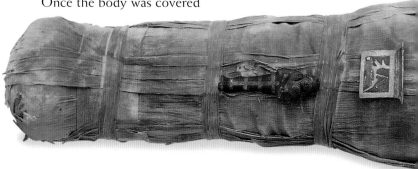

the underworld, a place full of poisonous snakes, executioners, and lakes of fire.

The journey to the tomb

After the coffin lid was closed, the priests invoked the gods' powers to help the mummy make it safely into the

canopic jars, the embalming leftovers, and goods the dead person would need in the afterlife – everything from food and fans to wine and wigs.

LOG ON.
www.ancientegypt.
co.uk/mummies/

COFFINS PROTECTED THE MUMMY FROM THIEVES AND EVIL MAGIC

kingdom of Osiris.

The coffin was placed on a wooden sled, and a boat carried it across the Nile River to the west bank, the place where the sun set and the dead lived. Oxen and men then dragged the sledge to the tomb. Ahead of the coffin walked mourners and priests who sprinkled milk and wafted incense. Behind it came a second sled carrying the

A procession of servants were also used to carry the goods to the tomb.

Brought back to life

Once inside the tomb, the coffin was stood upright and a solemn ritual called the Opening of the Mouth was performed by a priest. While incense burned, the priest touched the mummy's mouth so that it could speak and eat again. He touched the

THE INTESTINES, STOMACH, LIVER, AND LUNGS WERE PLACED IN SEPARATE CANOPIC JARS.

protection took their chances on the journey. But even they were buried with protective spells, as these were vital if a dead person was to have any hope of completing the trip.

The meaning of mummy

Mummy comes from the Arabic word *mummiya*. It has nothing to do with the word the English use for mother! *Mummiya* means bitumen, a type of sticky black tar. Why such an odd name to describe a preserved body?

eyes so that they could see, the nose so that it could breathe, and the ears so that they could hear. By restoring these senses, the body was reborn into a whole new existence. Once this was done, the tomb was sealed.

Mummies are worth it

To the ancient Egyptian mind, the long and elaborate process of mummification was well worth the effort. It was the best way to ensure a successful afterlife. The *ka* would now be able to recognize its well-preserved former body and nourish it, and the *ba* would treat it as its home as it traveled between the afterlife and the tomb.

Egyptians who couldn't afford embalming or even a coffin for

INCENSE BURNS AND MOURNERS WAIL AS PRIESTS PERFORM THE OPENING OF THE MOUTH CEREMONY.

It originated when the Arabs visited Egypt, long after the art of mummy-making had died out. They found some of the last bodies to be embalmed in Egypt, between about 500 BC and AD 400. This was a time when embalmers took less care over their work. In their hurry to prepare a corpse, they filled it with molten resin, which turned the body black all over.

This puzzled the Arabs, who wondered what could have been used to blacken a body. They could only think of one thing, *mummiya*, or bitumen. In time the word came into the English language where it was shortened to "mummy."

PYRAMID POWER

The pyramids of Giza are the largest stone buildings on Earth. They are precision-built supertombs, designed to house a king's mummy for eternity and send his soul straight to the stars. When they were new, and covered in dazzling white limestone, it must have seemed as though the gods themselves had created them. In fact, the pyramids were built by the people of the Nile Valley 4,500 years ago. Although we've learned a lot about them, many riddles remain.

THE SPHINX STANDS GUARD OVER THE PYRAMIDS OF GIZA. IT HAS THE BODY OF A LION AND THE FACE OF A KING.

Tomb story

The pyramids are unbelievably old. Even during the time of later pharaohs such as Tutankhamun, the pyramids were already ancient monuments. The kings who built them had become long-forgotten historical figures. But despite the extreme age of the pyramids, the story of Egyptian tomb-building began even before the Pyramid Age.

Mastaba tombs

A lot of big changes happened in Egypt in about 3100 BC. Lower and Upper Egypt united to become one country, and the age of the pharaohs began. Before this time, the dead were usually buried in simple pits in the desert. But after 3100 BC, custom-built, underground tombs with rooms became the fashion. To mark the tomb, a neat mound of mud bricks was

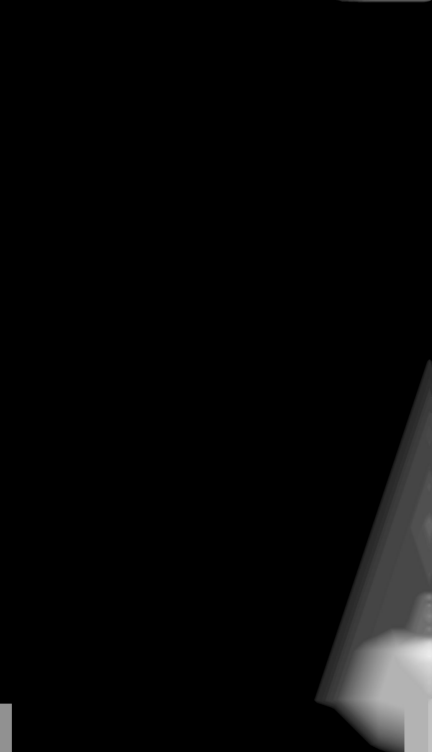

Granite Ball & Bronze Hook
found in the small chapels
from Queen's Chamber in the
Great Pyramid.
Discovered & Opened by
Waynan Dixon
in 1872.

THIS WORKMAN'S HOOK AND STONE POUNDER ARE THE ONLY OBJECTS EVER FOUND INSIDE THE GREAT PYRAMID, WHICH WAS ROBBED IN ANCIENT TIMES.

first pyramid. Because of its shape, it's known as the Step Pyramid – and you can still see it today.

The Pyramid Age

Djoser's Step Pyramid started a new trend. For the next 800 years the rulers of ancient Egypt built pyramids throughout the land. They were tombs fit for Egypt's kings.

At first, the pyramid builders made step pyramids, like Djoser's. Then, during the reign of the pharaoh Sneferu (2613–2589 BC), someone had

master – but not from mud bricks. Instead, he used stone. And Imhotep's inventiveness didn't stop there. On top of the king's mastaba he added a smaller stone platform, then a smaller one on top of that, and

THE PYRAMIDS OF GIZA HAD ALL BEEN BROKEN INTO BY 1000 BC

another and another.

Eventually the mound of stone rose up in a series of six huge steps. Perhaps it was meant to be a stairway to heaven, which King Djoser would climb after his death to join Ra, the mighty sun-god. Whatever it represented, this building was ancient Egypt's

the bright idea of building a smooth-sided or "true" pyramid. But the builders got their math wrong. Partway through building Sneferu's pyramid they realized the sides were far too steep. Questions were asked and heads were scratched. They couldn't knock it down and start again, so they changed the angle of the slope, which gave it a strange shape.

Sneferu was not too pleased with his tomb, which became known as the Bent Pyramid, so he had a second one built nearby, known as the Red Pyramid. This time the builders got it right. From then on, the craft of building smooth-sided pyramids reached new heights.

It was Sneferu's son, Khufu (reigned 2589–2566 BC), who created the most famous pyramid of all, at Giza, close to present-day Cairo. Made from some 2.3 million blocks of stone, each weighing around 2.5 tons, the Great Pyramid is the largest ever built, rising 481 ft (146 m) into the sky.

LOG ON...
www.pbs.org/wgbh/
nova/pyramid

P lanning the Great Pyramid

Before work began, Khufu's architects had to find the right

ARCHAEOLOGISTS HAVE DISCOVERED THAT THE GREAT PYRAMID WAS BUILT BY ABOUT 15,000 WELL-FED VOLUNTEERS, NOT BY SLAVES AS PREVIOUSLY THOUGHT.

43

place to build. They needed a large area of flat land, strong enough to support the weight of the massive building. They also needed building stone – lots of it. The flat limestone plateau at Giza was the perfect place. Next, they recruited thousands of laborers and organized them into teams at the building site. Some carved rock at the nearby quarries, while others worked on the pyramid itself. But how was such a building constructed without the use of trucks, drills, or cranes?

Toil, sweat, and tears

The millions of limestone blocks used in the Great Pyramid were cut using simple tools of stone, copper, and wood – the ancient Egyptians didn't have the advantage of iron tools at this time.

Blocks were moved from the quarries to the building site on wooden sleds, pulled by teams of sweating, shouting workers.

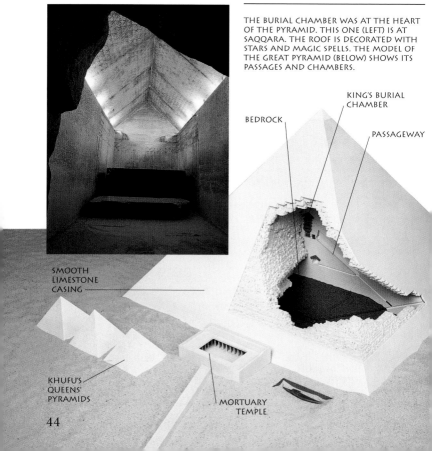

THE BURIAL CHAMBER WAS AT THE HEART OF THE PYRAMID. THIS ONE (LEFT) IS AT SAQQARA. THE ROOF IS DECORATED WITH STARS AND MAGIC SPELLS. THE MODEL OF THE GREAT PYRAMID (BELOW) SHOWS ITS PASSAGES AND CHAMBERS.

KING'S BURIAL CHAMBER

BEDROCK

PASSAGEWAY

SMOOTH LIMESTONE CASING

KHUFU'S QUEENS' PYRAMIDS

MORTUARY TEMPLE

The blocks then had to be lifted into place. Each chunk of stone weighed about the same as 40 adults, so it must have been a back-breaking job to haul them up the sides of the pyramid.
How they did it is one of the mysteries of ancient Egypt.

There's little doubt that a sloping ramp made from crushed stone and sand was used, but no one seems to know what shape it was. It might have been a long, straight ramp, a ramp that zig-zagged up one side, or even one that wrapped itself around all four sides of the pyramid.

ONE OF THE SHAFTS IN KHUFU'S BURIAL CHAMBER POINTS TOWARD THE CONSTELLATION OF ORION.

F inishing touches

When all the blocks were in place, the rough sides of the Great Pyramid were smoothed off with a layer of white, polished limestone. As this astonishing building neared completion, its tip may even have been crowned with a layer of gold.

All that was then needed was for the mummy of Khufu to be laid in his burial chamber, deep inside the pyramid.

P yramid precision

Even after 4,500 years, the Great Pyramid remains a masterpiece of geometrical design. Its four sides are aligned almost exactly with true north, south, east, and west. No one is sure how such accuracy was achieved using only primitive tools. The pyramid contains a complex system of passages, chambers, and shafts. In fact, the two shafts found in the king's burial chamber point directly toward constellations that were important to the ancient Egyptians – Orion and Sirius. The shafts were probably there to allow the king's soul to travel to the stars.

45

The pyramid effect

The Great Pyramid had a dramatic effect on Egyptian civilization. Building it had been such a vast enterprise that the whole country was mobilized into supplying labor, food, and stone. The work had needed such organization, resources, and willpower that it transformed Egypt into an efficient and powerful state – in fact, the world's first true state. This was an awesome achievement.

Pyramids perish

Trends come and go, which is what happened with pyramids. As tombs, they were never ideal. Pyramids were often still unfinished when their kings died, and they were rather obvious places to burgle. Pyramids were most popular among the rulers of the Old Kingdom (c.2686–2181 BC). The ones built after this time were smaller and less well made, and by the time of the New Kingdom (c.1550–1070 BC) a completely new type of tomb was in use for ancient Egypt's rulers.

THE PYRAMIDS OF GIZA WERE BUILT FOR THE PHARAOHS KHUFU, KHAFRE, AND MENKAURE. THE SMALLER PYRAMIDS WERE FOR THEIR CHILDREN AND QUEENS.

THE PYRAMIDS STILL INSPIRE
ARCHITECTS TODAY, THOUGH
NOW STEEL, CONCRETE, AND
GLASS ARE USED. THIS ONE
IS IN PARIS, FRANCE.

TOMB RAIDERS

Ancient Egyptian tombs weren't always easy places to break into. Some were protected by stone blocks, traps, and curses. Tombs were supposed to be safe places for the dead to rest in peace. But no burial place is truly safe – not if someone is really determined to raid the grave! In Egypt, pharaohs and ordinary folk both had the same worry – tomb raiders.

THIS GOLD MASK WAS FOUND IN TUTANKHAMUN'S TOMB. HIS BRIEF REIGN HAD BEEN FORGOTTEN BY EVERYONE, INCLUDING THE ROBBERS.

WEIRD WORLD
ROBBERS FOUND THE TOMB OF QUEEN NEFERTARI, THE MAIN WIFE OF PHARAOH RAMESSES II, AND STOLE ALMOST EVERYTHING, INCLUDING THE MUMMY'S BANDAGES. ALL THAT'S NOW LEFT OF THE POOR QUEEN ARE HER KNEES!

A grave business
Tomb robbers were a tough bunch. First, they had to break into a tomb, which often meant tunneling through solid rock. Then they had to avoid pits that had been dug to trap them. They also needed strong stomachs, because robbing the

ARCHAEOLOGIST HOWARD CARTER INSPECTS THE SECOND OF TUTANKHAMUN'S THREE COFFINS.

LOG ON...
www.national
geographic.com/egypt/

dead could be a gruesome job. It wasn't only grave goods the robbers were after – statues, furniture, and the like – they also wanted the very bandages from the mummy! It must have been like unwrapping a present, because the bandages concealed jewelry, precious amulets, and all kinds of small, portable treasures.

As tombs were filled with ever more valuable goods, tomb robbing increased. Robbers followed a simple rule – steal it, then sell it. Even though anyone caught in the act was put to death, the robbers weren't discouraged.

Robbing the afterlife

To the ancient Egyptians, disturbing the dead was the ultimate nightmare. They really believed that a person's life in the next world would be ruined if someone broke into their tomb, opened their coffin, and

ROBBERS ESPECIALLY WANTED SMALL ITEMS OF JEWELRY THAT WERE EASY TO HIDE AND SELL.

49

WEIRD WORLD
IN 1871, THE MUMMIES OF
ABOUT 40 PHARAOHS WERE
FOUND CRAMMED INTO ONE
TOMB. BECAUSE THEIR TOMBS
HAD BEEN DISTURBED BY
ROBBERS, A LATER PHARAOH
HAD COLLECTED THEIR
BODIES AND
RE-BURIED THEM.

worst of all, destroyed the tightly wrapped mummy in their haste to find treasure. Something had to be done. Most of all, the tombs of the pharaohs had to be protected.

The secret valley

The pharaohs of the New Kingdom were the first to come up with a plan to defeat the robbers. From about 1500 BC, they chose to be buried in a secret valley in the south of Egypt, far away from their traditional burial grounds at Saqqara and Giza. Today, this royal burial site is known as the Valley of the Kings. Over a period of about 500 years, some 60 pharaohs and nobles were buried there, in tombs cut into the rocky sides of the valley. Each tomb consisted of a sloping corridor with rooms leading off it. Some rooms were filled with grave goods, and one room contained the most precious item of all – the royal mummy, sealed inside a wooden coffin or a stone sarcophagus.

The one that got away

The Valley of the Kings was supposed to be safe from

THE WALLS OF TUTANKHAMUN'S BURIAL CHAMBER ARE DECORATED WITH SCENES SHOWING HIS FUNERAL AND HIS ARRIVAL IN THE AFTERLIFE.

thieving hands. Even though the entrances to the royal tombs were hidden, the robbers – often the same people who'd dug the tombs in the first place – found them and looted them … except for one. By a stroke of luck, the resting place of a long-forgotten king was not robbed. His name was Tutankhamun, and when his tomb was found in 1922, it revealed wonderful things about the lives and riches of the pharaohs.

Archaeologists like Howard Carter, who made this famous discovery, are themselves modern-day tomb raiders. But unlike the robbers who risked death to sell stolen treasures, archaeologists send their finds to museums for people to study and marvel at the wonders of ancient Egypt.

THE VALLEY OF THE KINGS WAS PERFECT FOR BUILDING ROCK-CUT TOMBS. IT ALSO HAD A NARROW ENTRANCE THAT COULD BE GUARDED AGAINST ROBBERS.

THE PHARAOH — GOD - KING OF EGYPT

For 3,000 years, ancient Egypt was ruled by kings and queens called pharaohs. From first to last there were about 170 of them, and each one ruled with enormous power. Most pharaohs were men, but on rare occasions Egypt was led by a woman. They were born as mortal people, but on the day they were crowned they were filled with divine power, and from then on they were gods living on Earth.

The keeper of order

People believed the pharaoh was chosen to carry out the gods' work on Earth. The pharaoh was a god-king, filled with the spirit of the hawk-headed god Horus, and was responsible for the well-being of the world. At important religious festivals he performed the temple rituals in person so the people could see him as a god-king. Ordinary Egyptians were in awe of him. The pharaoh was thought to be so powerful that it was dangerous even to touch him by accident.

THE PHARAOHS' JEWELRY WAS MADE IN ROYAL WORKSHOPS. THIS FINE GOLD CHEST ORNAMENT IS INLAID WITH GEMSTONES.

People were convinced he had the power to keep the whole universe in good working order – and that meant everything from running the government to controlling the Nile River's floods. Of course, the pharaoh couldn't really control the yearly flooding of the Nile, but

STATUES OF PHARAOHS PORTRAY THEM AS POWERFUL, GODLIKE BEINGS. HERE, THE PHARAOH MENKAURE, WEARING THE TALL WHITE CROWN OF UPPER EGYPT, IS PROTECTED BY TWO GODDESSES.

A ROYAL FAMILY – AKHENATEN, HIS QUEEN
NEFERTITI, AND THREE OF THEIR SIX
DAUGHTERS. HE WAS A DARING KING WHO
TRIED TO BANISH THE OLD GODS.

the ancient Egyptians didn't
know that. So, in years when
the floods were low – people
called these "bad Niles" – the
pharaoh was blamed. A
disaster, such as a poor harvest,
reminded people how
important the pharaoh's role
was in daily life. In short, it was
his duty to protect the world. If
he didn't, people feared the
world would plunge into chaos.

The leader of the people

It's not easy for us to grasp
what it meant to be a pharaoh,
since we're dealing with ideas
that seem alien to our modern
way of thinking. However, the
rest of the pharaoh's job
description is pretty
straightforward.

The pharaoh was Egypt's
head of state. As leader of the
government he controlled the
army, the law, and the cults of
all the gods. To help him
govern he had thousands of

priests, overseers, and officials who took care of Egypt's day-to-day administration. Among them were the viziers, or chief ministers. Viziers were the "chiefs of all the king's works" and were men with a lot of political power.

The pharaoh ruled his people from his royal palaces where he lived with his family. His ministers brought him news about what was happening in the country, and important foreign visitors came to see him.

Royal strength

If a pharaoh reigned for 30 years, a *sed* festival was held in his honor. This was a royal jubilee, during which the pharaoh "died," was reborn, and then went through a second coronation ceremony. It was designed to renew the pharaoh's strength, giving him new power to carry on the task of looking after Egypt. The highlight of the *sed* festival was when the pharaoh ran along a course to prove his fitness to rule.

The royal regalia

A pharaoh had many items of regalia. He had crowns of different shapes and colors, and a striped headcloth that came down over his shoulders. On his forehead he wore a symbol of the cobra goddess Wadjet, whom people believed would spit flames at any enemies. In his hands the pharaoh held a hook-shaped scepter, which symbolized his kingship, and a flail, which

WEIRD WORLD

PHARAOHS WORE FALSE BEARDS TIED TO THEIR CHINS WITH CORDS. A BEARD WAS A SIGN OF A PHARAOH'S GODLIKE NATURE. EVEN WOMEN PHARAOHS WORE FALSE BEARDS!

RAMESSES THE GREAT RULED EGYPT FOR 67 YEARS. HIS LONG REIGN IS NOTED FOR ITS MANY GRAND BUILDINGS.

symbolized Egypt's fertility. The pharaoh even had a royal swatter for shooing away flies!

Choosing a wife

As the king of Egypt was believed to be descended from the gods, it was difficult to know who was good enough to be his queen. He could have many wives, but his queen (known as Great Royal Wife) had to be royal, so the blood of the gods was not diluted. For this reason kings sometimes married their sisters or a close female relative.

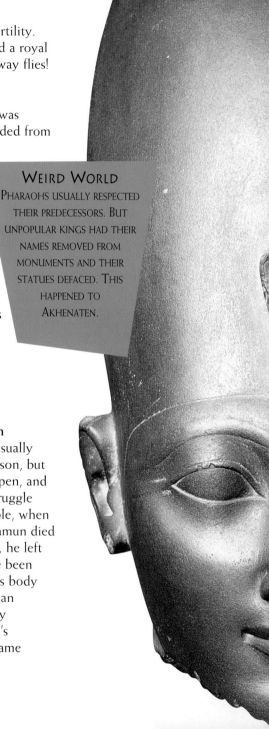

WEIRD WORLD
PHARAOHS USUALLY RESPECTED THEIR PREDECESSORS. BUT UNPOPULAR KINGS HAD THEIR NAMES REMOVED FROM MONUMENTS AND THEIR STATUES DEFACED. THIS HAPPENED TO AKHENATEN.

The royal succession

The role of pharaoh usually passed from father to son, but this didn't always happen, and sometimes a power struggle took place. For example, when the pharaoh Tutankhamun died young, aged about 19, he left no sons. He may have been assassinated. While his body was being embalmed, an elderly vizier called Ay married Tutankhamun's widow, and so he became Egypt's next pharaoh.

The female pharaoh, Queen Hatshepsut, was another ruler who did not come to power in the usual way. When her husband, Tuthmosis II, died, her son was too young to become pharaoh, so she made herself "king" of Egypt. Hatshepsut ruled wisely and built up Egypt's economy instead of making war.

LOG ON... www.eyelid.co.uk/

The god-king

The word pharaoh comes from the ancient Egyptian *per-aa*, or "great house," meaning the palace where the king lived. Over the years, the sense of the word changed, until by about 1350 BC it came to refer to the king himself. The pharaoh had many titles, chief of which was Lord of the Two Lands – a reminder that Egypt had been formed by joining the lands of Upper and Lower Egypt. Another of his grand titles was Son of Ra, which was a way of saying he was the child of Amun-Ra, the sun god. It meant the pharaoh was more than a king – he was a god.

HATSHEPSUT WAS A VERY DETERMINED WOMAN WHO RULED EGYPT FOR 20 YEARS.

57

TEMPLES — HOMES OF THE GODS

Ancient Egyptian temples were awesome structures. The grandest of them had giant statues, colorful walls, and vast halls lined with carved stone columns. Temples were central to the lives of the Egyptians, many of whom worked in temple farms and workshops.

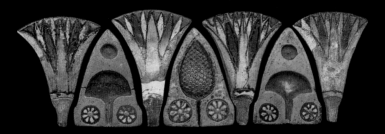

The purpose of temples

Ancient Egyptian temples were quite different from today's churches, synagogues, and mosques. They were not meeting places for worshippers, but real, earthly homes for the gods. People believed the spirits of Egypt's gods actually lived and moved inside these sacred places.

Temples were also the centers for the religious cults that grew up around the gods. An important god would have a temple that might expand over time to become a huge

THE LOTUS FLOWER WAS A NATIONAL SYMBOL IN ANCIENT EGYPT. COLUMNS IN TEMPLES WERE OFTEN CARVED TO RESEMBLE LOTUS PETALS OR PAPYRUS LEAVES.

complex containing offices, farms, schools, libraries, and workshops. Temples were "living buildings" in every sense – they were continually enlarged and rebuilt, usually on the same spot.

Step inside a temple

If you were an ordinary Egyptian, you wouldn't have

THE TEMPLE OF DENDERA IS DEDICATED TO THE GODDESS HATHOR, WHOSE FACE GAZES OUT FROM ITS ENTRANCE.

WEIRD WORLD

AT SOME TEMPLES, WATER
WAS POURED OVER
STATUES. PEOPLE
THOUGHT IT ABSORBED
MAGICAL POWERS AND
COLLECTED IT FOR USE
AS MEDICINE.

STONE SPHINXES LINE THE
AVENUE LEADING UP TO
THE TEMPLE AT LUXOR.

WEIRD WORLD
THE GREAT HYPOSTYLE HALL AT
THE TEMPLE OF AMUN-RA,
KARNAK, CONTAINED 134
MASSIVE STONE COLUMNS.
HYPOSTYLE IS FROM A
GREEK WORD MEANING
"RESTING ON PILLARS."

been allowed very far inside a temple. Your place was in the outer courtyards with the other lowly members of the public. Only priests and priestesses – the officials who lived and worked at the temple – could enter the heart of the building itself.

A large temple had a series of halls linked by a long corridor. As priests walked from hall to hall, they passed through "forests" of stone columns before reaching the temple's holiest place.

The holy of holies

The darkest, most holy room was located toward the far end of the temple, where the floor sloped upward and the ceilings became lower. A raised area inside the room symbolized the Egyptian creation story, in which the world was born as a sacred hill, rising from the ocean that surrounded it. Priests

anointed it with oil, dressed it in clean clothes, and adorned it with jewelry. Then he left gifts of food and sweet-smelling incense. This was to make the statue attractive to the god, so that he or she would live inside it. The priests believed these actions would protect the pharaoh, the people, and the world the Egyptians knew.

Sacrifices to the god

Animals were sacrificed as gifts to the god. The Greek historian Herodotus described a sacrifice he had witnessed. Wine was poured over a cow as an offering to the god. Then a priest slit the animal's throat, and removed its head, which was sold in the market or thrown into the Nile. The carcass was stuffed with bread, honey, figs, and spices. Finally, the sacrifice was coated in oil and roasted while the priests chanted prayers. Once the god had "eaten" the meat, the priests would finish it. The smells of roasting sacrifices, incense, and smoke from torches must have given the temple a heady atmosphere.

approaching this room imagined they were on a journey to the hill of creation itself. It was a deeply mystical experience for them.

Respect for the god

Inside the temple's holiest room was a statue of the god of the temple. Three times a day, at dawn, midday, and evening, the high priest washed the statue,

THIS IS A PRIEST CALLED SEMATAWY. HE IS HOLDING A STATUE OF THE GOD ATUM.

61

MAGIC SPELLS AND MEDICINE

The main gods of ancient Egypt played little part in everyday life, so ordinary people turned to magic to solve common problems. Their magic had nothing to do with making things appear and disappear. For the Egyptians, it was a form of medicine, just like a doctor's potions and powders. In fact, magic and medicine were linked very closely togethe

THE ANKH WAS A POPULAR MAGIC CHARM.

CORIANDER

CUMIN SEEDS

CASTOR OIL

THE EGYPTIANS HAD A WIDE KNOWLEDGE OF HERBS AND THEIR MEDICINAL REMEDIES.

Good spells, bad spells

Ancient Egyptians were convinced magic worked, and conjured it up by the use of spells. People relied on magic to cure or ward off every type of day-to-day worry, such as disease, injury, and the risks of giving birth. They wore magic charms, or amulets, to heal themselves and keep danger away. They used spells to pass messages to ghosts, if a dead relative was upset or causing trouble.

Spells were also used to cause harm. These were curses. A person might write their enemy's name on a pot,

WEIRD WORLD
HEADLICE WERE TREATED WITH CASTOR OIL AND OX FAT. THIS STOPPED LICE FROM BREEDING AND SUFFOCATED THEM!

A YOUNG NOBLEMAN IS PURIFIED WITH LIFE-GIVING WATERS AND SURROUNDED BY ANKH AMULETS.

SCARAB AMULETS
WERE PLACED OVER A
DEAD PERSON'S HEART
TO HELP THEM
THROUGH THE
WEIGHING OF THE
HEART CEREMONY.

or make a clay figure of them. Then, by smashing the object while uttering the spell, they hoped something nasty would befall the enemy.

Powerful plants

The Egyptians had a detailed knowledge of healing plants, which they used hand in hand with magic. Today, science has shown us that many Egyptian remedies were genuinely effective. Garlic was very popular – it was used to prevent colds and flu. Coriander aided digestion, cumin eased the pain of arthritis, and castor oil was taken as a laxative.

The magic of death

Coffins and mummies' bandages are full of evidence of the Egyptians' magic beliefs. Most rich Egyptians were buried with a copy of the Book of the Dead. This was a type of magical route map to the afterlife, filled with spells to

protect a dead person on the long journey. Some of the most powerful spells were written on amulets. For example, amulets known as heart scarabs were inscribed with a spell to stop a dead person's heart from speaking out against them during the Weighing of the Heart ceremony (a type of afterlife entrance exam). An outspoken heart might condemn its owner and ruin the chance of an afterlife. Placing heart scarabs between a mummy's bandages was thought to prevent this nightmare.

WEIRD WORLD

HEADACHES AND PRESSURE ON THE BRAIN WERE RELIEVED BY TREPANNING – CUTTING A HOLE THROUGH THE SKULL TO EXPOSE THE GRAY MATTER ITSELF!

Doctors and knowledge

Doctors were important people in ancient Egypt, and they practiced magic and medicine in equal amounts. Doctors knew a lot about the body and had some good ideas about what made it ill. They believed that people were born healthy, and would not fall ill or die unless influenced by a harmful force. Science and magic came together to defeat this force through a mixture of medicines and spells.

Although there were no microscopes to see viruses and bacteria, doctors guessed that diseases came from wormlike creatures invading the body. They also understood that the heart "speaks out" through the head and hands – a reference to the pulse. In spite of this advanced knowledge, they believed the heart, not the brain, controlled intelligence and emotions. That's why embalmers preserved the heart, and threw the brain away!

Medicine and healing

The Egyptians wrote down much of their medical wisdom on scrolls. One such scroll contains 877 different ways to treat various illnesses and disorders, some of which are still used. Raw meat was applied to cuts (it prevents bleeding), and dressings were made from moldy bread (it stops the spread of harmful bacteria). Wounds were sewn up with needles and thread. Often, doctors only expected remedies like these to relieve pain. Magic would provide the real cure.

A BRONZE SITULA (A TYPE OF BUCKET) WAS USED FOR SPRINKLING HOLY WATER – THOUGHT TO HAVE POWERFUL HEALING PROPERTIES.

65

EVERYDAY LIFE

Most people in ancient Egypt led busy lives. There was plenty of work to do, in fields, quarries, and workshops throughout the land. The working day lasted for up to twelve hours, from dawn till dusk. But people didn't work all the time – they had fun playing games and socializing. At religious festivals and public celebrations, entertainers danced and made music. Everyday life was a mixture of work and pleasure.

Happy New Year!

The Egyptian year began in mid-June, when the Nile River began to flood. As this event gave a new life to the land, it was a good time to say a new year had begun. There were twelve months in the year, which was divided into three seasons – flood, spring, and harvest. Each season had four months, and there were three weeks in each month. A week had ten days in it, which meant each month had thirty days.

Planting the fields

In October, after the flood waters had subsided, it was time for the farming year to begin. Farmers marked out their small fields in the fresh mud left by the river, then scattered emmer (a primitive kind of wheat) and

VILLAGES IN EGYPT TODAY HAVE CHANGED LITTLE SINCE ANCIENT TIMES. THEY STAND NEXT TO THE NILE, AND BUILDINGS ARE STILL MADE FROM MUD BRICKS.

barley seeds. Farm animals were let into the fields to trample the seeds into the soil, burying them out of sight of hungry birds. Everyone in the family, young and old, was expected to help the animals and get stamping, too. The emmer-wheat crop was Egypt's staple food, and it had to be tended and nurtured until it was time to harvest it in April and May.

THIS MODEL SHOWS A MAN'S CATTLE BEING COUNTED TO FIND OUT HOW RICH HE IS.

Animals on the farm

The most important farm animal was the cow. It was not only a source of meat and milk, it was also used for work on the farm. The number of cattle a person owned was a measure of their wealth. At the start of their meat, wool, and hides. Their skins, when sewn up, were used to transport water. Poultry – geese, ducks, and chickens – were kept for their eggs. Pigs were also kept, but people thought they were unclean. If you were a pig

HUNTING LIONS IN THE DESERT WA A FAVORITE SPORT OF PHARAOHS

each new year, government officials counted everyone's cattle – the more a person had the more tax they had to pay. Sheep and goats were raised for farmer, you were looked down upon by everyone! Donkeys carried heavy loads, such as grain baskets. At harvest time they trampled on the grain to remove the husks.

Fruit and vegetables

Farmers were the most important workers in Egypt, producing vast amounts of food to feed the large population. Their fields looked like small, square plots, a little like the gardens we see around towns today. Apart from cereals, they grew onions, leeks, garlic, peas, lentils, beans, radishes, cabbages, cucumbers, and lettuces. Many fruits were grown, too, such as red grapes, figs, dates, and pomegranates.

FARMERS GREW MANY DIFFERENT TYPES OF FRUITS, VEGETABLES, CEREALS, AND HERBS IN THEIR FIELDS ALONG THE NILE RIVER.

Food and drink

What would you have eaten in the days of the pharaohs? That depended on your place in society. The poor made do

AFTER PICKING THE GRAPES, WORKERS CRUSHED THEM BY TREADING. THE JUICE WAS THEN COLLECTED IN CLAY JARS.

with bread, a few vegetables (mainly onions), fruit, and beer. This was the basic diet for adults and children. Beer, made from barley, was a thick, soupy liquid. It was nutritious, and not very alcoholic. It was also safer to drink than Nile water, since this might be infected with parasitic worms and other bugs – but no one realized that at the time. As for meat, the poor trapped hares, fish, and wildfowl.

Meat from oxen, and wine, were two luxuries that only the rich enjoyed with their daily meals. One thing eaten by both rich and poor was sand, which got blown into bread dough. Sometimes it was even added to flour to make it easier to gind! The worn teeth of mummies are the telltale signs that the Egyptians chewed gritty bread.

Houses made from mud

Architecture in ancient Egypt came in two different varieties. Grand buildings of stone, such as pyramids and temples, were at one extreme, and people's homes, made from sundried mud bricks, were at the

LOG ON...
www.ancientegypt.co.uk/life/

other. Even royal palaces were built using mud bricks. Stone buildings were made to last, but people's houses were made from the same mud that farmers used to grow their crops. And when the Nile River flooded, it washed some of the buildings away, recycling the bricks back into mud. Did the people mind? No doubt they accepted it as part of life and set about rebuilding their homes each year with new bricks. Houses were small, and often joined together in groups that shared walls. Inside were one or two living rooms and a kitchen with a hearth. Most were single-story buildings, but in cities houses were sometimes several stories high. Roofs never changed – they were always flat.

Games and toys

Life wasn't all work and no play. The ancient Egyptians found time to let their hair down. They liked to play board games, especially one called *senet*, which means "passing." The lucky winner made it through the underworld to the afterlife, but the loser didn't. Other games were more like sporting events, such as wrestling matches and stick fighting, played at religious festivals. Children played with balls and spinning tops, and models of people and animals.

Song and dance

Music and dancing were important in religious and temple life, and also in non-religious celebrations such as

A COUPLE PLAYING SENET MOVE PIECES AROUND A BOARD OF SQUARES. THE ROUTE THE PIECES TOOK SYMBOLIZED THE JOURNEY TO THE AFTERLIFE.

banquets. Musicians were both male and female. They blew flutes and other pipes, plucked the strings of harps, and shook bells, cymbals, and rattles. Dancers were usually women or young girls, who sometimes quickly as they do now! Most clothes were made from linen, a cloth woven from the fibers of the flax plant. Wool was rarely used. Egyptian clothes were simple – a loincloth or kilt for men, and a close-fitting

PAINTINGS IN TOMBS SHOW THAT EGYPTIANS LOVED A GOOD PARTY!

performed in pairs. They did cartwheels and handstands and they learned their energetic dance routines by heart.

Clothes and hairstyles

Just as our taste in clothes and hairstyles changes, so it did for the ancient Egyptians – though fashions didn't come and go as dress or loose wrap for women. Clothes were usually left white, but some were dyed with plant and mineral extracts to decorate them red, blue, and yellow.

On their feet people wore sandals made from palm leaves and rushes. Leather sandals were comfortable and lasted longer, but were expensive.

FARM WORKERS CUT OFF THE EARS OF WHEAT AND BARLEY WITH COPPER SICKLES, THEN CARRIED THEM FROM THE FIELDS IN BIG BASKETS.

Egyptian heads were adorned with wigs made from real human hair. A good wig was a status symbol, rather like the "right" pair of shoes is today. Wigs were shown off at public events.

Children, especially boys, had their heads shaved, except for a side patch where their hair was left long. This was the "sidelock of youth," and it showed that the child was not yet thought of as an adult.

J ewelry

Ancient Egypt was a nation of craftspeople, as well as farmers. Craft workers of extraordinary skill carved stone for statues, pressed clay to make pots, and worked with metals and semiprecious stones to create fabulous jewelry. Gold was the most valued of all metals used in making jewelry.

CROCODILES MADE THE NILE AND ITS BANKS DANGEROUS FOR EVERYONE, BUT CROCS WERE CONSIDERED SACRED ANIMALS.

Because it did not tarnish gold was said to be a divine metal – the very flesh of Ra, the sun god. The connection with the gods made it the ideal metal to use in funerals.

THIS NECKLACE HAS AMULETS IN THE SHAPE OF COWRIE SHELLS, FALSE BEARDS, AND FISH. IN THE CENTER IS HEH, THE GOD OF INFINITY.

Tombs were filled with golden objects, and pharaohs, like Tutankhamun, had masks of solid gold. Lesser people had masks of cartonnage (linen and papyrus stiffened with plaster). These were covered in a wafer-thin layer of gold.

Beads and amulets were made from stones such as green feldspar, red jasper, and dark blue lapis lazuli – a stone that came from the region that is now Afghanistan. Lapis was rare and expensive, and a cheaper substance, called faience, was often used instead. Faience was a blue or green paste that could be shaped and fired like pottery.

An Egyptian family

How would you like to get married at 12? That's the age girls were expected to marry in ancient Egypt. Boys married at 15. Some Egyptians waited until they were a little older. But not that much older, since

THESE COURTIERS APPEAR TO HAVE CONES TIED TO THEIR HEADS. THE CONE MAY HAVE BEEN A SYMBOL TO INDICATE THAT A PERSON WAS NICELY PERFUMED.

BRACELETS WERE WORN AROUND THE WRISTS, LIKE THIS ONE MADE FROM GOLD AND LAPIS LAZULI.

No school!

The only schools in ancient Egypt were run by temples, and these were usually only for boys from wealthy homes. Very few children ever went to school. The government didn't do much to educate the people. After all, if boys were taught to be farmers, brick makers, carpenters, jewelers, tomb builders (and tomb robbers) by their fathers, that was all the education they needed.

As for girls, their mothers taught them all they

people weren't expected to live to a ripe old age – most were lucky if they made it to their forties. The purpose of marriage was to produce children.

Parents wanted children since it was the duty of offspring to look after their mother and father as they grew old. Families often had as many as ten children, and it was the mother's job to bring them up. However, when boys were old enough their fathers took over, training them to be their assistants at whatever work they did.

needed to know about looking after a family and home.

The few privileged boys were given lessons in reading, writing, mathematics, and astronomy. Because they were literate – they knew how to read and write – they had a high status in society. These boys became the next generation of priests, scribes (clerks), and governors – the people needed to run the country.

75

IMAGES IN WRITING

n July 1799, French soldiers found a remarkable object buried in the sand near the Egyptian village of Rashid, whose old name was Rosetta. The large slab of black stone they uncovered was the key to unlocking one of the world's greatest riddles – how to read hieroglyphs, the writing of ancient Egypt. Until this discovery, hieroglyphs had been a mystery for 1,400 years.

SCRIBES CHOSE THEIR SCRIPT IMAGES FROM THE WORLD AROUND THEM. THE OWL REPRESENTS THE LETTER "M".

Cracking the code

For years, people had tried and failed to read hieroglyphs. But when the Rosetta Stone was unearthed, Thomas Young (1773–1829), an Englishman who could read 14 languages by the age of 12, realized it could help decipher the Egyptians' long-forgotten writing. The stone was carved with an identical inscription in two different languages – Egyptian (using two different scripts, or writing styles) and Greek.

Young compared the Greek with the Egyptian and slowly began to decode the strange signs and symbols. He hoped to be the first person to make sense of Egyptian writing. Eventually, it was a Frenchman, Jean-François Champollion (1790–1832), who made the

> **WEIRD WORLD**
>
> WRITING FROM RIGHT TO LEFT SEEMS THE WRONG WAY TO US, BUT THIS WAS THE WAY MANY ANCIENT LANGUAGES WERE WRITTEN, AND IT'S STILL USED FOR HEBREW AND ARABIC TODAY.

THE ROSETTA STONE IS AN ELABORATE LETTER OF THANKS WRITTEN TO PHARAOH PTOLEMY V, IN 196 BC.

real breakthrough. By matching royal names in the Greek and Egyptian scripts, Champollion used his knowledge of Greek to work out what hieroglyphs stood for. In 1822, he finally solved the puzzle.

SOME HIEROGLYPHIC SIGNS NEEDED A LOT OF PRACTICE BY SCRIBES AND ARTISTS ALIKE. HERE, AN ARTIST HAS GOT CARRIED AWAY DRAWING A DUCKLING.

Hieroglyphic confusion

The hieroglyphic script came into use about 3100 BC. It was a system of writing in signs, which represented a mixture of sounds (as the letters of our alphabet do) and whole words. Other signs were used to clarify the meaning of a word, so it

wouldn't be misread. For most of ancient Egyptian history there were about 700 hieroglyphic signs, but by the end of the civilization there were about 6,000.

Hieroglyphs could be read from left to right, or from right to left. They could be written in rows or in columns. If this sounds confusing, it was! Hieroglyphic writing was deliberately kept complicated, so that few people could use it, and the scribes could maintain their high status in society. Most people in ancient Egypt couldn't read or write.

Holy hieroglyphs

In ancient Egypt, writing, like so many other things, was thought to be of divine origin. It was the gift of Thoth, the god of writing and knowledge. The Egyptians called their writing *medu-netjer*, which means "the god's words." Later, the ancient Greeks called it *hieroglyphikos grammata*, meaning "holy signs," from which we get the word hieroglyphs. Because they were sacred, hieroglyphs were used mainly for religious purposes. They were painted on coffins, and carved in stone on the walls of temples and tombs.

Rapid writing

Hieroglyphs represented the most formal way to write, but they weren't ideal. The signs were tricky, and slow to draw. Busy scribes needed an easier,

A SCRIBE OFTEN HAD TO TRAVEL ON OFFICIAL BUSINESS. HE TOOK A WATER POT, REED PENS, AND INK, WHICH FIT INTO A WOODEN CASE, LIKE THIS ONE.

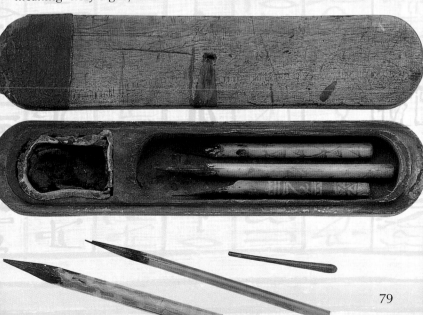

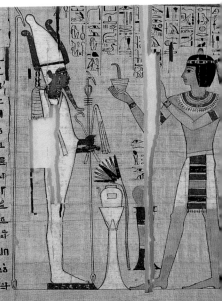

ON PAPYRUS, SCRIBES NORMALLY USED THE FAST FORM OF WRITING, HIERATIC. HERE, HIEROGLYPHS HAVE ALSO BEEN USED ABOVE A SACRED IMAGE OF OSIRIS.

faster script for everyday use, and developed one called hieratic, from a Greek word meaning "priestly." Hieratic was a shorthand for hieroglyphs, and became the main script for business and private records.

By about 600 BC, an even simpler script came into use. This one was called demotic, from a Greek word meaning "popular." Popular it might have been, but it's still thought that only one in every 100 people could read and write! Demotic is descended from hieroglyphs, but it's almost impossible to see any resemblance. The Rosetta Stone's message was written in demotic, as well as Greek and hieroglyphs.

Scribes

Scribes were those trained to read and write. They inherited their jobs from their fathers,

THE PAPYRUS REED GREW ALONG THE NILE. IT WAS USED TO MAKE WRITING PAPER, ROPE, AND BOATS.

and learned their craft by copying out texts over and over again. Their education started at age nine and lasted for about five years. Scribes had to study hard and were beaten if they were lazy. But their years of training were worth the effort. Scribes were privileged, and did not have to pay tax.

sprinkled a few drops of water as an offering to the god Thoth. Taking up his reed pen, he dipped it into his water pot then rubbed it over a block of dried ink – soot for black, ochre (a mineral) for

LOG ON...
http://touregypt.net/ename/

THE MOST FAMOUS OF ALL SCRIBES, IMHOTEP, WAS MADE INTO A GOD

Writing, paper, and ink

When he wrote, a scribe sat cross-legged on the ground. He pulled his kilt tight against his knees, making a flat surface on which to work. He wrote on paper made from the stems of the papyrus reed. The soft pith of the reed was cut into strips, placed in two layers, then pounded together to form a strong sheet.

Before he got scribbling, a scribe

red – and began to write, brushing the ink onto his papyrus scroll. Both hieratic and demotic scripts were written from right to left. Because the ink took a time to dry, a right-handed scribe had to be very careful not to smudge his writing as he worked across the scroll.

Scribes were trained professionals and their work was usually neat and easy to read. It's from their words and records, as much as from mummies and tombs, that we know so much about life in ancient Egypt.

IMHOTEP WAS A TALENTED SCRIBE WHO ALSO DESIGNED THE FIRST PYRAMID, AT SAQQARA.

ANIMAL MUMMIES

The ancient Egyptians mummified animals with the same care they took when preserving people. Cats, dogs, cows, and fish were embalmed if they were associated with particular gods, or favorite pets, or simply needed for food in the afterlife. Toward the end of ancient Egyptian civilization, large cults grew up around certain animals, creating a massive demand for animal mummies for dedication to the gods.

CATS WERE SACRED TO THE GODDESS BASTET. FOR KILLING A CAT, THE PUNISHMENT COULD BE DEATH.

WEIRD WORLD
IN THE 1800S, HUNDREDS OF TONS OF MUMMIFIED CATS WERE SHIPPED TO LIVERPOOL, ENGLAND, TO BE GROUND UP AND USED AS FERTILIZER ON FARMS!

THE EGYPTIANS WERE THE FIRST PEOPLE TO TAME AFRICAN WILD CATS AND KEEP THEM AS PETS.

Afterlife menu

The Egyptians believed that dead people needed food in the next life, so supplies were buried with them. Roasts of meat, whole birds, and fish were preserved, wrapped in bandages, and placed inside wooden coffinettes (little coffins) in the shape of the food. Some of these mummies were painted a brown color, to make them appear roasted and ready to eat!

THIS GOLD CONTAINER HOLDS THE MUMMIFIED BODY OF AN IBIS. THESE BIRDS WERE DEDICATED BY THE MILLIONS TO THOTH, THE GOD OF SCRIBES AND WRITING.

A pet is not just for life

Egyptians loved their pets, and often wanted to take them to the afterlife. When their owners died, cats, dogs, gazelles, monkeys, and even ducks were buried in their owners' tombs. No one knows if a pet was killed and given the mummy treatment as soon as its master died, or whether it was allowed to live out its natural life.

Animals with gods inside

Some animals were singled out for special treatment because people thought the spirits of the gods lived inside them. This was particularly true of a sacred bull known as the Apis Bull, of which there was only ever one at a time. This animal was kept in luxury beside a temple, attended by servants and a harem of cows. When it died, it was embalmed with enormous care and ceremony. After removing its organs and placing them in giant canopic

83

CROCODILES WERE SACRED TO THE GOD SOBEK. SOME TEMPLES KEPT TAME CROCS IN POOLS, AND THEY WERE FED FINE FOOD.

jars, the body was filled with bags of sawdust and natron. It was then bandaged and buried with full honors.

A nimal mummy industry
Toward the end of ancient Egyptian history, from about 300 BC until about AD 400, animals were mummified in vast quantities. Pilgrims could buy all kinds of creatures to give to the gods. Falcons, dogs, jackals, baboons, scorpions, snakes, crocodiles, and even scarab beetles were available as mummies. Some may have been "farmed" to provide a constant supply of bodies to the profitable mummy-making industry. An animal cemetery at Saqqara still contains an estimated four million ibis mummies, each in its individual burial jar. About 10,000 were buried there every year for some 400 years!

WEIRD WORLD
MUMMIES THOUGHT TO BE HUMAN BABIES SOMETIMES TURNED OUT TO BE HAWKS, A BIRD SACRED TO THE GOD HORUS. THEY WERE BABY-SIZED AND WORE MASKS WITH HUMAN FACES.

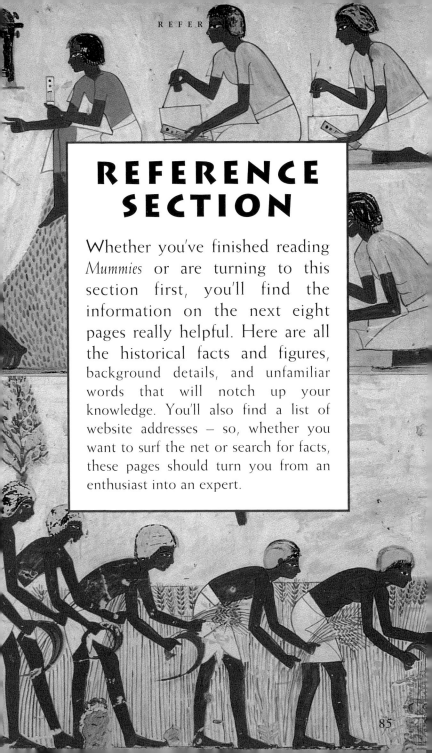

REFERENCE SECTION

Whether you've finished reading *Mummies* or are turning to this section first, you'll find the information on the next eight pages really helpful. Here are all the historical facts and figures, background details, and unfamiliar words that will notch up your knowledge. You'll also find a list of website addresses – so, whether you want to surf the net or search for facts, these pages should turn you from an enthusiast into an expert.

ANCIENT EGYPT TIMELINE

Ancient Egyptian history is traditionally divided into three large parts, known as the Old, Middle, and New Kingdoms. There are also several smaller parts, known as periods. The 170 or so pharaohs who ruled ancient Egypt over the course of 3,000 years are ordered into 31 dynasties or groups. This simplified table lists the dynasties, their approximate dates, and year(s) when the pharaohs reigned.

PRE-DYNASTIC PERIOD
5500–3100 BC

EARLY DYNASTIC PERIOD
3100–2686 BC
1st Dynasty 3100–2890 BC
Narmer (3100 BC)
Aha (3100 BC)
Djer (3000 BC)
Djet (2980 BC)
Den (2950 BC)
Anendjib (2925 BC)
Semerkhet (2900 BC)
Qa'a (2890 BC)

2nd Dynasty 2890–2686 BC
Hetepsekhemwy (2890 BC)
Raneb (2865 BC)
Nynetjer
Weneg
Sened
Peribsen (2700 BC)
Khasekhemwy (2686 BC)

OLD KINGDOM
2686–2181 BC
3rd Dynasty (2686–2613 BC)
Sanakht (2686–2667 BC)
Djoser (2667–2648 BC)
Sekhemkhet (2648–2640 BC)
Khaba (2640–2637 BC)
Huni (2637–2613 BC)
4th Dynasty 2613–2494 BC
Sneferu (2613–2589 BC)
Khufu (2589–2566 BC)
Djedefre (2566–2558 BC)
Khafre (2558–2532 BC)
Menkaure (2532–2503 BC)
Shepseskaf (2503–2498 BC)
5th Dynasty 2494–2345 BC
Userkaf (2494–2487 BC)
Sahure (2487–2475 BC)
Neferirkare (2475–2455 BC)
Shepseskare (2455–2448 BC)
Raneferef (2448–2445 BC)
Nyuserre (2445–2421 BC)
Menkauhor (2421–2414 BC)
Djedkare (2414–2375 BC)
Unas (2375–2345 BC)
6th Dynasty 2345–2181 BC
Teti (2345–2323 BC)
Userkere (2323–2321 BC)
Pepi I (2321–2287 BC)
Merenre (2287–2278 BC)
Pepi II (2278–2184 BC)
Nitiqret (2184–2181 BC)

FIRST INTERMEDIATE PERIOD
2181–2055 BC
7–8th Dynasties 2181–2125 BC
Many minor pharaohs
9–10th Dynasties 2160–2025 BC
Many minor pharaohs
11th Dynasty 2125–2055 BC
Mentuhotep I

Intef I (2125–2112 BC)
Intef II (2112–2063 BC)
Intef III (2063–2055 BC)

MIDDLE KINGDOM

2055–1650 BC
11th Dynasty (continued)
2055–1985 BC
Mentuhotep II (2055–2004 BC)
Mentuhotep III (2004–1992 BC)
Mentuhotep IV (1992–1985 BC)
12th Dynasty 1985–1795 BC
Amenemhet I (1985–1955 BC)
Senusret I (1965–1920 BC)
Amenemhet II (1922–1878 BC)
Senusret II (1880–1874 BC)
Senusret III (1874–1855 BC)
Amenemhet III (1855–1808 BC)
Amenemhet IV (1808–1799 BC)
Queen Sobeknerfu (1799–1795 BC)
13th Dynasty 1795–1650 BC
About 70 minor pharaohs

SECOND INTERMEDIATE

PERIOD 1750–1550 BC
14th Dynasty 1750–1650 BC
Some minor pharaohs
15th-16th Dynasties 1650–1550 BC
Sheshi
Khyan
Apepi I
Khamudi
17th Dynasty 1650–1550 BC
Intef VII
Taa I
Taa II
Kamose (1555–1550 BC)

NEW KINGDOM

1550–1069 BC
18th Dynasty 1550–1295 BC
Ahmose I (1550–1525 BC)
Amenhotep I (1525–1504 BC)
Thutmose I (1504–1492 BC)

Thutmose II (1492–1479 BC)
Thutmose III (1479–1425 BC)
Queen Hatshepsut (1473–1458 BC)
Amenhotep II (1427–1400 BC)
Thutmose IV (1400–1390 BC)
Amenhotep III (1390–1352 BC)
Amenhotep IV (Akhenaten)
(1352–1336 BC)
Smenkhkare (1338–1336 BC)
Tutankhamun (1336–1327 BC)
Ay (1327–1323 BC)
Horemheb (1323–1295 BC)
19th Dynasty 1295–1186 BC
Ramesses I (1295–1294 BC)
Seti I (1294–1279 BC)
Ramesses II (1279–1213 BC)
Merneptah (1213–1203 BC)
Amenmessu (1203–1200 BC)
Seti II (1200–1194 BC)
Siptah (1194–1188 BC)
Queen Tausret (1188–1186 BC)
20th Dynasty 1186–1069 BC
Sethnakhte (1186–1184 BC)
Ramesses III (1184–1153 BC)
Ramesses IV (1153–1147 BC)
Ramesses V (1147–1143 BC)
Ramesses VI (1143–1136 BC)
Ramesses VII (1136–1129 BC)
Ramesses VIII (1129–1126 BC)
Ramesses IX (1126–1108 BC)
Ramesses X (1108–1099 BC)
Ramesses XI (1099–1069 BC)

THIRD INTERMEDIATE

PERIOD 1069–747 BC
21st Dynasty 1069–945 BC
Smendes I (1069–1043 BC)
Amenemnisu (1043–1039 BC)
Psusennes I (1039–991 BC)
Amenemope (993–984 BC)
Osorkon the elder (984–978 BC)
Siamun (978–959 BC)
Psusennes II (959–945 BC)

continued overleaf

22nd Dynasty 945–715 BC
Sheshonq I (945–924 BC)
Osorkon I (924–889 BC)
Sheshonq II (890 BC)
Takelot I (889–874 BC)
Osorkon II (874–850 BC)
Takelot II (850–825 BC)
Sheshonq III (825–773 BC)
Pamai (773–767 BC)
Sheshonq V (767–730 BC)
Osorkon IV (730–715 BC)
23rd Dynasty 818–715 BC
Pedibastis I (818–793 BC)
Sheshonq IV (780 BC)
Osorkon III (777–749 BC)
24th Dynasty 727–715 BC
Bakenrenef (727–715 BC)

LATE DYNASTIC PERIOD
747–332 BC
25th Dynasty 747–656 BC
Piy (747–716 BC)
Shabaka (716–702 BC)
Shabitku (702–690 BC)
Taharka (690–664 BC)
Tanutamun (664–656 BC)
26th Dynasty 664–525 BC
Necho I (672–664 BC)
Psammetic I (664–610 BC)
Necho II (610–595 BC)
Psammetic II (595–589 BC)
Apries (589–570 BC)
Ahmose II (570–526 BC)
Psammetic III (526–525 BC)
27th Dynasty 525–404 BC
Cambyses (525–522 BC)
Darius I (522–486 BC)
Xerxes I (486–465 BC)
Artaxerxes I (465–424 BC)
Darius II (424–405 BC)
Artaxerxes II (405–359 BC)
28th Dynasty 404–399 BC
Amyrtaeus (404–399 BC)
29th Dynasty 399–380 BC

Nefarites I (399–393 BC)
Hakor (393–380 BC)
Nefarites II (380 BC)
30th Dynasty 380–343 BC
Nectanebo I (380–362 BC)
Teos (362–360 BC)
Nectanebo II (360–343 BC)
31st Dynasty 343–332 BC
Artaxerxes III (343–338 BC)
Arses (338–336 BC)
Darius III (336–332 BC)

THE GRECO–ROMAN PERIOD
323–310 BC
Alexander the Great (332–323 BC)
Philip Arrhidaeus (323–317 BC)
Alexander IV (317–310 BC)

PTOLEMAIC PERIOD 310–30 BC
Ptolemy I Soter (305–285 BC)
Ptolemy II Philadelphus
(285–246 BC)
Ptolemy III Euergetes I
(246–221 BC)
Ptolemy IV Philopator
(221–205 BC)
Ptolemy V Epiphanes (205–180 BC)
Ptolemy VI Philometor
(180–145 BC)
Ptolemy VII Neos Philopator
(145 BC)
Ptolemy VIII Euergetes II
(170–116 BC)
Ptolemy IX Soter II (116–107 BC)
Ptolemy X Alexander I (107–88 BC)
Ptolemy IX Soter II (restored)
(88–80 BC)
Ptolemy XI Alexander II (80 BC)
Ptolemy XII Neos Dionysos
(80–51 BC)
Ptolemy XIII (51–47 BC)
Ptolemy XIV (47–44 BC)
Queen Cleopatra VII (51–30 BC)
Ptolemy XV Caesarion (44–30 BC)

FAMOUS PHARAOHS

Narmer
REIGNED: 3100 BC
FAMOUS FOR: being the first pharaoh
He united the kingdoms of Upper and Lower Egypt.

Djoser
REIGNED: 2667–2648 BC
FAMOUS FOR: the first pyramid
He built the Step Pyramid, at Saqqara.

Khufu
REIGNED: 2589–2566 BC
FAMOUS FOR: the Great Pyramid
Despite building the Great Pyramid at Giza, not a lot is known about Khufu. He must have been a powerful ruler, since the building of his pyramid would have involved mobilizing the whole country.

Queen Hatshepsut
REIGNED: 1473–1458 BC
FAMOUS FOR: peace and trade
Hatshepsut was originally appointed Egypt's regent – to look after the throne until Thuthmosis III was old enough to become pharaoh. But she had herself crowned and for a time she was pharaoh in her own right.

Akhenaten
REIGNED: 1352–1336 BC
FAMOUS FOR: banishing the gods
This pharaoh worshipped Aten, the god represented by the disc of the sun. He named himself Akhenaten ("glory of the sun disc") and founded a new capital city called Akhetaten. There, a new, less formal style of art developed. Akhenaten abandoned the old gods and closed their temples. He wanted people to worship only one god – Aten.

Tutankhamun
REIGNED: 1336–1327 BC
FAMOUS FOR: his burial treasures
A minor pharaoh who became king at the age of nine, he was Akhenaten's son. Tutankhamun changed Egypt's religion back to the worship of many gods. In 1922, his tomb was found in the Valley of the Kings, untouched by robbers.

Ramesses II
REIGNED: 1279–1213 BC
FAMOUS FOR: buildings and battles
Known as Ramesses the Great, his 67-year reign is marked by the building of temples and statues, and by a famous battle against the Hittites. The Battle of Qadesh (c.1274 BC), in modern-day Syria, was inconclusive, and Ramesses signed the world's first peace treaty. He had more than 100 children.

Queen Cleopatra VII
REIGNED: 51–30 BC
FAMOUS FOR: being the last pharaoh
When Cleopatra VII became pharaoh, her family, the Ptolemys, had ruled Egypt for about 250 years. They were Greeks, not native Egyptians. Cleopatra ruled Egypt with help from the Romans. She killed herself by making a snake bite her, after which Egypt became part of the Roman Empire.

THE MAIN GODS

Amun, Amun-Ra

GOD OF: creation; king of the gods
LOOKS LIKE: a man wearing a crown
with two tall feathered plumes
Became the supreme god during the
New Kingdom and was worshipped
throughout Egypt. His greatest
temple was at Karnak. His name
means Hidden or Invisible One.

Aten

GOD OF: daylight and warmth
LOOKS LIKE: the disc of the sun
whose rays ended in human hands
This sun god rose to prominence
during the reign of Akhenaten.
Aten's popularity only lasted a few
years, and when Akhenaten died,
people lost interest in this god.

Anubis

GOD OF: embalming
LOOKS LIKE: a jackal, or a jackal-
headed man
According to myth, it was Anubis
who wrapped the body of the
murdered Osiris. It was because of
this that he became associated with
mummification.

Bastet

GODDESS OF: joy; the home; the
warmth of the sun
LOOKS LIKE: domestic cat or a woman
with the head of a cat
The center of her cult was at Bast, a
town to the northeast of Cairo,
where a great temple was built in her
honor. Large cemeteries of
mummified cats have been found
close to her temple.

Horus

GOD OF: the sky; the rising sun,
eternal life; keeper of order
LOOKS LIKE: a hawk, or a man with
the head of a hawk
He was the son of Osiris and Isis and
was closely identified with the living
pharaoh. His name means the
Distant One.

Isis

GODDESS OF: fertility; nature
LOOKS LIKE: a woman with the
hieroglyph for her name (a throne)
on her head
She was both the wife and the sister
of Osiris, and the mother of Horus.
Because she had helped restore the
body of the murdered Osiris, she
was seen as the goddess of the dead.
She was a popular goddess,
worshipped throughout Egypt.

Osiris

GOD OF: the afterlife; the dead; the
fertile land
LOOKS LIKE: a green-faced mummy
wearing a crown of ostrich feathers
He was the husband and the brother
of Isis, and the father of Horus.
Osiris was the first king to survive
death, and became the ruler of the
afterlife, where he kept order among
those who journeyed there. He
bore the regalia of a king – the
crook and flail.

Ra, Re

GOD OF: creation; father of the gods
LOOKS LIKE: a man with the head of a
hawk (or a ram) wearing a

sun-disc headdress
Ra was the most important god in ancient Egypt. He was a sun god who was worshipped from the beginning of Egyptian history. Every ruler called him or herself the "Son of Ra." It was believed that after a pharaoh died he or she joined Ra in the heavens, traveling with him through the skies in a solar barque (sun boat).

Seth

GOD OF: chaos; storms; evil
LOOKS LIKE: an unidentified animal, something like a wild boar
He was the brother of Osiris, whom he murdered, and for this reason he was seen as the bringer of bad luck. He was referred to as the "lord of deserts and foreign lands."

Thoth

GOD OF: wisdom; writing, reading, mathematics; magic
LOOKS LIKE: a baboon, or an ibis, or a man with the head of an ibis
The god of scribes, Thoth is usually shown holding a reed pen and a writing palette. The ibis may have been his symbol because its long curved beak looked like a pen. He was the inventor of writing and language. He was also also the moon god, which meant he controlled the calendar and time itself.

ANCIENT EGYPT WEBSITES

www.clpgh.org/cmnh/exhibits/ egypt/index.html
Life in ancient Egypt, based on displays at the Carnegie Museum of Natural History, Pittsburgh, Pa.
www.discovery.com/guides/ ancientworlds/egypt/egypt.html
Daily life, pyramids, and recent archaeological discoveries
www.si.edu/resource/faq/nmnh/ mummies.htm
Mummies and how they were made
www.discovery.com/news/features /animalmummies/animalmummies. html
All about animal mummies
www.cmi.k12.il.us/Urbana/ projects/cybermummy/
Unlocks the secrets of this Roman Period Egyptian mummy
http://cs.oberlin.edu/classes/cs115 /lect29n.html
The Rosetta Stone and the deciphering of hieroglyphs
www.friesian.com/tombs.htm
Detailed maps and plans of tombs in the Valley of the Kings
http://www.sis.gov.eg/egyptinf/ history/html/sport001.htm
Ancient Egyptian sports
http://guardians.net/hawass/index. htm
Official website of the archaeologist in charge of the Giza monuments
www.guardians.net/egypt/kids/ index.htm
Excellent website, with several links and general information
www.ancientegypt.co.uk
The British Museum ancient Egypt site
http://showcase.netins.net/web/ ankh/index.html
General Egypt site, good graphics

GLOSSARY

Akh
The part of a person's identity believed to live in the afterlife, formed when the *ba* and the *ka* were reunited.

Amulet
Object used as a protective device or lucky charm to ward off evil.

Ankh
Hieroglyph for the word meaning "life," shaped like a cross with a looped head.

Ba
A person's spirit or soul, thought to live on after death. The *ba* is often shown as a human-headed bird.

Book of the Dead
Collection of about 200 spells, placed with the mummy to help the dead person reach the afterlife safely.

Canopic jars
Four jars that held the mummified stomach, liver, lungs, and intestines of a dead person.

Cartonnage
Material made from linen stiffened with plaster, used to make mummy masks and coffins.

Coffin
Container in which a mummified body was placed, usually made from wood or cartonnage.

Coffinette
Small coffin in the shape of the mummy inside it, such as an animal.

Crown
Item of regalia worn by the pharaoh to symbolize his rule over Egypt. There were several different crowns.

Demotic
Style of handwriting which developed from the hieratic script and which could be written quickly.

Deshret
Name the ancient Egyptians called the desert that lay beyond their land. It meant "Red Land," after the color of the sand.

Dynasty
Series of pharaohs from related families. Egypt's pharaohs formed 31 dynasties.

Emmer
Type of wheat commonly grown in ancient Egypt.

Faience
Material formed from a paste of crushed quartz which had a glazed surface. It was fired hard in a kiln, and was used to make small objects such as amulets.

Hieratic
Form of handwriting which was developed from hieroglyphs and was quick to write.

Hieroglyphs
The oldest writing script used in ancient Egypt, consisting of signs that refer to the meaning and sound of words.

Inundation
The period when the Nile River flooded each year – between June and September.

Ka
Life force or "double" of a living person, formed at birth. After death, the *ka* lived in the dead person's tomb where it survived, provided there were offerings left there for it.

Kemet
Ancient Egyptian name for Egypt. It meant "Black Land," after the color of the mud deposited by the Nile River when it flooded.

Lapis lazuli
Highly prized dark blue stone from Afghanistan, used in ancient Egypt for amulets and jewelry.

Lower Egypt
The northern region of ancient Egypt.

Mastaba
Rectangular bench-shaped tomb with a flat roof.

Mummy
Preserved body. In ancient Egypt human and animal bodies were artificially mummified by drying them out with natron, then wrapping with linen bandages.

Natron
A type of salt that occurred naturally in Egypt and which was used to dry bodies during the process of mummification.

Obelisk
Tall stone with a pyramid-shaped top that was a symbol of the Sun's rays.

Opening of the Mouth
Ceremony performed on mummies to restore them to life.

Papyrus
Water reed used to make a type of writing paper, baskets, ropes, sandals, and medicine. Its root could be eaten, or burned as fuel.

Pharaoh
King or queen of ancient Egypt.

Pyramid
Tomb with a square base and four sloping sides, built to hold the mummified body of a pharaoh.

Saqqara
Burial ground near Memphis (south of Cairo), used for royal and private burials.

Sarcophagus
Stone coffin. The word is from the Greek for "flesh-eater."

Scribe
Person trained to read and write.

Sed **festival**
Festival for renewing a pharaoh's divine strength, held in the 30th year of his reign.

Senet
Board game similar to today's game of checkers, played on a board of 30 squares.

Sidelock of youth
Long lock of hair on children who were not yet old enough to be thought of as adults.

Sphinx
Creature with a lion's body and human head, particularly that of the pharaoh.

Thebes
Capital of Egypt during the New Kingdom.

Upper Egypt
The southern region of ancient Egypt.

Valley of the Kings
Burial site used during the New Kingdom for the burial of pharaohs in rock-cut tombs.

Vizier
The chief minister, and the highest official in the government. He kept the king informed on all matters.

Weighing of the Heart
When a dead person's heart was weighed against a feather, to see if they were worthy of entering the afterlife.

INDEX

A

afterlife 20–23, 30,
    64, 83
Akhenaten, Pharaoh 54,
    56, 89
Alexander the Great 35
ammonite 26
Ammut, goddess 22, 23
amulets 24, 36, 49, 62,
    64, 74
Amun-Ra, sun god 24,
    27, 57, 60, 90
animal-headed gods 25,
    28
animals, sacred 73, 82,
    83
ankh 62
Anubis, god 7, 22, 25, 28,
    90
Apis Bull 83
architecture 70–71
Asia 11–12
Atacama Desert 11
Atum, god 61
Ay, vizier 56

B

ba 21, 23, 32, 38
bandages 31, 35–36,
    49, 64
Bastet, goddess 28, 82, 90
beads 74
beards, false 55
beer 69
Bent Pyramid 42–43
boats 14, 18, 20
body scanner 12, 13
Book of the Dead 21,
    39, 64
brain 32, 65
bread 70
burial 8, 11, 12, 13,
    37–38
    chambers 44, 51
    pits 30, 31, 40

C

calendar 67
canopic jars 32, 37,
    38
Carter, Howard 49, 51
cats 28, 82
cattle 67, 68
cemeteries 12, 37,
    41, 84
Champollion, Jean-
    François 76–78
China 12
Cleopatra, Pharaoh
    89
clothes 72
coffins 8, 12, 36, 51
    nests of 34, 49
columns, stone 60
crafts 73
crocodiles 73
crops 67, 69
crowns 18, 52, 55
curses 48, 62–64

D

dancing 71 72
death 20 21
demotic script 80
Dendera 58
desert 17
desert mummies 11 12,
    30–32
diseases 64 65
Djoser, King 41–42, 89
doctors 64
duality 17

E

Egypt, state of 46
embalming 9, 13, 30,
    32–35
emmer 67
everyday life 66–75

F

families 74–75
farming 16, 67–69, 73
festivals 52, 55, 66, 71
Field of Reeds 20
food 69–70, 83
frozen mummies 9–12
funerals 37–38, 74

G

games 66, 71
Giza 40, 43–44, 45
gods and goddesses 22,
    24–28, 52, 62, 74, 90–91
gold 34, 35, 45, 48, 52,
    73–74, 75
government 54–55, 75
grave goods 37, 49, 51, 74
Great Pyramid 43–46

H

hairstyles 73
Hall of Two Truths 22
Hathor, goddess 58
Hatshepsut, Queen 57, 89
headlice 62
heart 34
heart scarabs 64
herbs 62, 64
Herodotus 61
hieratic script 80
hieroglyphs 18, 76–79
holy water 59, 65
Horus, god 27, 52, 84
    Eye of 24, 27, 91
houses 67, 70

I

ibis 83, 84
Ice Man 9
Ice Princess 12–13
Imhotep 41–42, 81
incense 36, 38, 61
Isis, goddess 27, 90

J, K

jackal 28
jewelry 30, 36, 49, 52, 73–74, 75
ka 22–23, 32, 38
Karnak 60
Khafre, Pharaoh 46
Khufu, Pharaoh 43, 45, 46
kurgans 12

L

laborers 43, 44
lapis lazuli 31, 74, 75
legends 27–28, 60–61
life cycle 20–21
lotus flower 58
Luxor 60

M

magic 21, 38, 39, 44, 62–65
marriage 75
masks 48, 74, 84
mastaba tombs 41–42
meat 69
medicine 59, 62–65
Memphis 18
Menkaure, Pharaoh 46, 52
mud bricks 40, 71
mummies 9–11, 31
mummies, Egyptian 9, 13, 18–19, 30–39
  animals 13, 82–84
  legends of 27–28
  making 32–36
mummy, meaning of word 38–39
music 71–72

N

Narmer, Pharaoh 18, 89
natron 34, 36
Nefertari, Queen 48
Nefertiti, Queen 54
New Kingdom 32, 46, 51
Nile River 14–17, 19, 28, 32, 54, 67, 71

O

Old Kingdom 46
Opening of the Mouth ceremony 37–38
organs 11, 32–33, 38
Orion 45
Osiris, god 25, 26, 27, 90

P

palaces 55, 71
papyrus 80, 81
Pazyryk nomads 12
peat bog mummies 10–11
pens 79
pets 13, 83
pharaohs 18, 52–57, 89
Peru 10, 11
priests 37, 55, 60, 61, 75
pulse 65
pyramids 16, 40–47

Q, R

queens 46, 52, 56
Ra (Re), sun god 25, 27, 42, 74, 90
Ramesses the Great, Pharaoh 18, 55, 89
Red Pyramid 43
regalia 55–56
religion 26, 52, 58–61, 82
Rosetta Stone 76, 80

S

sacrifices 61
sandals 72
Saqqara 41, 44, 84
sarcophagus 36, 51
scarabs 25, 64, 84
schools 75
scientific methods 13
scribes 75, 79, 80–81
scrolls 65
sed festival 55
Seth, god 27, 91
senet game 71

shroud 32
Siberia 12
situla 65
sleds 37, 44
Sneferu, Pharaoh 42–43
South America 11
sphinxes 40, 60
star constellations 45
statues 18, 52, 61
Step Pyramid 41–42

T

Taklamakan Desert 12
temples 16, 18, 26, 58–61
Thebes 27
Thoth, god 22, 23, 24, 79, 81, 83, 91
timeline 86–88
Tollund man 9
tomb robbers 31, 42, 48–51
tombs 16, 18–23, 40–41, 46, 51, 74
tools 42, 44
Torrington, John 11
toys 71
trepanning 64
Tutankhamun, Pharaoh 6, 48, 49, 51, 56, 74, 89
Tuthmosis II, Pharaoh 57

U, V

underworld 17, 20–23, 36
Valley of the Kings 51
villages 67
viziers 55

W, Y

Wadjet, goddess 55
websites 91
Weighing of the Heart 22, 64
wigs 73
wine 69
work 66, 75
writing 76 81
Young, Thomas 76

CREDITS

Dorling Kindersley would like to thank:
Almudena Diaz and Nomazwe Madonko for DTP assistance.
Thanks also to Chris Bernstein for the index.

Picture Credits

The publisher would like to thank the following for their kind permission to reproduce their images:
Position key: a=above; b=bottom; c=center; l=left; r=right; t=top.

Owen Beattie:
University of Alberta 11br;

Bolton Museum:
10bl;

Bridgeman Art Library, London / New York:
David Roberts, City of Bristol Museum and Art Gallery: 59, Giraudon/Louvre, Paris, France: 7, 63;

British Museum:
3, 4, 21t, 22b, 23b, 24tr, 24bl, 26l, 27c, 28l, 30bl, 31b, 33c, 34b, 36tl, 36b, 38tl, 39b, 42tl, 43b, 49br, 55, 56-57, 58, 61bc, 62tl, 64tl, 65, 70c, 74c, 74bl, 77, 78, 78-79, 79, 80cl, 80t, 81, 82b, 83, 84, 88c, 92c; Peter Hayman 1, 8tl;

Cairo Museum:
6, 48c;

Corbis:
Richard T. Nowitz 16bl; Sygma 35br;Sygma/Viennareport Agency 8b;

Alistair Duncan, Egyptian Museum Cairo: 14cr, 17tr, 19c, 25b, 29c, 50c, 51tr, 53, 54-55, 67tr, 68b, 90c;

Mary Evans Picture Library:
49t;

Werner Forman Archive:
44cl; Egyptian Museum, Cairo 54;

Ronald Grant Archive:
13cr;

Images Colour Library:
Michael Howell 64-65;

Jurgen Liepe:
66b;

Manchester Museum:
20bc, 30cr, 52, 72t;

NASA: 15c;

Science Photo Library:
Geoff Tompkinson 12tr; John Sandford 45tr;

Silkeborg Museum, Denmark:
9tr;

Getty Images, Stone:
Richard Passmore 60-61.

Book Jacket Credits:
Front cover: Ardea London Ltd.